D1252726

(

ST FRANCIS
OF ASSISI

ST FRANCIS
OF ASSISI

A Pictorial Biography

by

Leonard von Matt
and Walter Hauser

Translated from the German by
Sebastian Bullough, O.P.

LONGMANS GREEN & COMPANY
LONDON · NEW YORK · TORONTO

LONGMANS, GREEN AND CO LTD
6 & 7 CLIFFORD STREET LONDON WI
BOSTON HOUSE STRAND STREET CAPE TOWN
531 LITTLE COLLINS STREET MELBOURNE

LONGMANS, GREEN AND CO INC
55 FIFTH AVENUE NEW YORK 3

LONGMANS, GREEN AND CO
20 CRANFIELD ROAD TORONTO 16

ORIENT LONGMANS LTD
CALCUTTA BOMBAY MADRAS
DELHI VIJAYAWADA DACCA

This Edition first published in 1956
Second impression 1957

IMPRIMI POTEST
Fr. Hilarius Carpenter, O.P., *Prior Provincialis*
Londini, die 15a Maii, 1955

NIHIL OBSTAT
Joannes M. T. Barton, S.T.D., L.S.S., *Censor deputatus.*

IMPRIMATUR
E. Morrogh Bernard, *Vic. Gen.*
Westmonasterii, die 28a Maii, 1955

PLATES PRINTED BY IMAGO, ZURICH
TEXT PRINTED IN GREAT BRITAIN BY
HAZELL WATSON AND VINEY LTD
AYLESBURY AND LONDON

CONTENTS

ACKNOWLEDGEMENTS

Illustrations, presentation and general design: Leonard von Matt, Buochs, Switzerland. All the photographs were taken by him during 1951 and 1952 specially for this work.

Text: The Rev. Walter Hauser, Parish-Priest at Sisikon, Uri, Switzerland.

Historical advisory committee: Fr Albert Ghinato, O.F.M., Professor of Franciscan History at the Pontifical Athenaeum "Antonianum", Rome; Fr Joseph Abate, O.F.M. Conv., Professor in the Pontifical Faculty of the Franciscan Conventuals, Rome; Fr Laurence Casutt, O.F.M. Cap., Member of the Capuchin Historical Institute in Rome.

Design on the cover: Toni Flüeler, after the altar-piece in the Cathedral of Città di Castello (cf. Plates 146 and 153).

Maps: Alwin Kneubühler.

This English translation, based on the original German language edition, is issued by arrangement with the original publishers: NZN Buchverlag, Zürich.

This work appears also in French, Italian and Dutch editions, and a separate edition is published in Western Germany.

THE COMING OF FRANCIS

Whoever would write of Francis must begin by asking the good God to give him a warm heart and that true simplicity, without which the task would be impossible.

Francis was the son of a rich cloth-merchant, Pietro Bernardone, and his wife, Donna Joanna Pica. He was born in 1181 or 1182, and his coming was like the coming of a fresh spring breeze to a tired world.[1]

It was whispered in the alleyways and squares of Assisi that this child was not born in any of the rich apartments of his home. It was said that his mother, as she lay in travail, full of apprehension of a difficult birth, asked to be taken down to the stable, where almost immediately she brought forth a very healthy boy. Thus already at his birth Francis resembled Our Blessed Lord in his poverty, for Our Lord also had begun his earthly life in a stable.[2]

Pietro Bernardone, when his firstborn son was born, was away in France, engaged upon business in order to increase his already considerable wealth. It is the opinion of many, that it was on a previous visit to France that he first met Donna Pica—Joanna was apparently her baptismal name—the daughter of a noble family of Picardy. Thus it was that in this couple nobility and riches made a match.

Notes on the four plates that follow

I   VIEW ALONG THE VALLEY OF THE TESCIO TOWARDS THE
HILL-TOWN OF ASSISI
Of all the rocky heights of Umbria none has so impressive a crown as Assisi with its rock-
fortress.

2   AN ALLEYWAY IN ASSISI
Today, as of old, the town, built of yellow and red stone, creeps up the hill to the powerful
fortress on the summit. The houses stand huddled together, and each house has three arched
doorways on the street: one is the entrance to the house, another leads to a stable or to a shop,
while the third, normally bricked up, was only used to carry out the dead.

3   SAN FRANCESCO PICCOLO
The stable where Francis was born has been turned into a chapel.

4   A CORNER IN ASSISI
We see in this man, carrying two waterpots, a symbol of Francis bearing through the dusty
streets of the world living water, "springing up into life everlasting".

[2]

2 3

HIS YOUTH

A man's earthly life begins at his birth, but the spiritual life that leads to eternity begins at his baptism. The son of Pietro Bernardone was taken to the church of Santa Maria Maggiore at Assisi to be baptized, and on his mother's instructions was named John after the Baptist, a presage indeed of the great preacher that he too was to become. But when Pietro came back from France, he gave him the name Francis, so as to keep in his own son a perpetual souvenir of France, the land he loved so well, and whose language Francis learned as a small child at home.[3]

Francis was sent to a school adjoining the church dedicated to the warrior-saint, St George, patron of knights. Here he learned Latin, and as soon as he left school his father began to teach him another skill, one in which he himself excelled; that of making money. Francis learned quickly, but he also quickly discovered how to spend it. His was a friendly and generous nature, and soon he became the darling of the town; the young people flocked after him, and in the evening the streets would often echo the sound of his merrymaking with his friends. Yet he never fell into any of the excesses which so easily tempt a young man with too much money. On one occasion his mother, upon being told of some spendthrift behaviour of her son, remarked prophetically: "All the same, I always hope he will turn out a real child of God after all."[4]

One day Francis was in his father's shop, when a beggar came in, asking for alms. Although the man begged in the name of Christ, he was roughly dismissed. He was hardly out of the door, when Francis reproached himself severely: "If this beggar had asked for something in the name of some great lord of this world," he said to himself, "I'm sure I would not have turned him out. But he asked me in the name of Christ—how could I be so hard-hearted?" And he would not rest until he had found the beggar and made him a gift. From then on, he never turned anyone away who begged in the name of Christ.[5]

God indeed hid from the wise and prudent what he had in store for Francis, and revealed it to the simple. For there was a well-known simpleton in the town, who used to run up to Francis in the street and spread his cloak on the ground before him, crying out: "*Pax et bonum!* Peace and goodness!" But he ceased his cries after the saint's conversion.[6]

Notes on the four plates that follow

5 SAN RUFINO

The basilica was begun in 1140, but various circumstances hindered its completion, and it was not until 1228 that the high altar was consecrated by Gregory IX. The cathedral was consecrated in 1253 under Innocent IV.

6 SAN RUFINO, THE WEST FRONT AND THE TOWER

7 SAN RUFINO, THE NORTHERN ROSE-WINDOW AND ARCADE

8 THE FONT, WHERE FRANCIS AND CLARE WERE BAPTIZED

Until the cathedral of San Rufino was ready, this font stood in the episcopal church of Santa Maria Maggiore (see Plates 32, 39, 40). Still, today, the children of the blessed city of Assisi are baptized at this font at San Rufino.

8

THE INDEPENDENCE OF ASSISI

When Francis was a young man, the world around him was full of wars. The Emperor at his anointing always received the commission to wield his sword in defence of the Church, but, in fact, the Emperor, pursuing his own ends, not infrequently turned his arms against her. The cities of Italy took sides and there were innumerable local wars. Moreover, the rising merchant class of wealthy citizens began to exert their power against the imperial nobility. At Assisi the local lord, a German count most devoted to the imperial cause, lived in the formidable castle or Rocca, and he now in his turn became the object of the townsfolk's resentment. When Innocent III, that great defender of the Church's rights, ascended the papal throne, the German Count of Assisi decided to visit the new pontiff at Narni, to pay him homage. While he was away the citizens of Assisi rose up and wrecked his fortress, and to this day the ruins that crown the hill bear witness to the havoc that they wrought there. They then hurriedly strengthened and heightened the walls of the city against future attack; at the same time they fell upon the city houses of any of the imperial nobles and set most of them on fire. The imperial party at Assisi now invoked the powerful aid of neighbouring Perugia, and the armed forces of Assisi and Perugia met at Ponte San Giovanni, where Assisi was hopelessly defeated.

Notes on the four plates that follow

9   VIEW FROM THE ROCCA MINORE TOWARDS THE ROCCA
    MAGGIORE AND THE UPPER PART OF THE CITY
    The fortress became to the citizens of Assisi a symbol of foreign domination, and they rose up
    and destroyed it.

10 VIEW FROM THE FORTRESS WALLS OVER THE PLAIN OF ASSISI

11 THE LATER MEDIEVAL TOWERS OF THE FORTRESS, SEEN FROM
    THE WEST
    These towers were built by Cardinal Albornoz in 1365 on the foundations of part of the old
    fortress which had been destroyed in 1198.

12 A SECTION OF THE OLD CITY WALLS
    The walls had been strengthened at the time of the destruction of the Rocca. It may well be
    that the young Francis took part in this rebuilding.

[6]

9

PRISONER AT PERUGIA

Among the prisoners taken at Ponte San Giovanni and marched into Perugia through the Arch of Augustus in 1202, there was also Francis, who had taken part in the battle. Although he was but a merchant's son, his education and wealth warranted his accommodation with the prisoners of noble birth. And here, even in the sorry circumstances of imprisonment, his irrepressible gaiety showed itself. But his companions felt that gaiety was out of place, and that the proper state of mind for a knight committed to prison was one of suitable mourning, and they reproached him for his levity. They hardly understood him when he simply said: "Didn't you know that a glorious future lies ahead of me? I know for certain that one day all the world will do me homage."[7]

One of the imprisoned knights was so arrogant and disagreeable that the others could hardly endure his conversation, but Francis went to him and talked with him in such a loving way that eventually he succeeded in making peace between them all.

Notes on the four plates that follow

13 THE ARCH OF AUGUSTUS AT PERUGIA
This is the main gate in the Etruscan walls, which date from the third or second century before
Christ. It was probably through this gate that Francis was taken into Perugia as a prisoner.

14 VIEW OVER THE ROOFS OF PERUGIA NORTHWARDS

15 SANT' ANGELO AT PERUGIA
This church, dating from the 5th or 6th century A.D., was already a much frequented sanctuary
in the time of Francis.

16 THE EAST DOORWAY OF THE PALAZZO DEI PRIORI AT PERUGIA
The Palazzo was begun in 1293 and completed in 1443. This was of course after the time of
St Francis, but the building belongs to the springtime of the Franciscan world.

[8]

13

14   15

FRANCIS SETS OFF TO BECOME A KNIGHT

The months of captivity at Perugia left Francis in weak health, and he fell gravely ill, so much so that for a time he lay at death's door. He recovered, however, and then the first time he went out the world somehow looked different to him; it had for the moment lost its glamour.

But soon he had regained his strength and returned to his usual gaiety. Yet there was a new seriousness about him, and he was preparing to leave for the wars in Apulia, in the company of a certain nobleman, in order there to merit the full status of knighthood. His preparations were elaborate and his equipment magnificent.

Just before his departure he met a certain knight who, though evidently of noble birth, was hard put to it to conceal his dire poverty. Francis made a sudden generous gesture and gave to this knight all his own gorgeous apparel.[8]

That night he had a dream; he dreamed that a voice called him by name and that he was led into a room containing an enormous array of weapons of war and military equipment. Francis asked to whom these belonged, and was surprised to learn that they belonged to him. This dream urged him to leave at once for Apulia, in search of the honours of chivalry, which now seemed so certainly within his grasp. It was scarcely day, when he and his friend rode out of the city. They reached Spoleto, and here again Francis had a dream; this time the voice asked him whither he was going. He answered without hesitation that he was going to Apulia to get his knighthood. The voice then said: "Which is it better to serve, the master or the servant?" Francis said: "The master, of course." The voice answered: "Then why do you serve the servant instead of the master, the poor instead of the rich?" Then Francis knew who was speaking. "Lord," he said, "what do you want me to do?" "Go home," came the answer, "there you will be told what to do."[9]

Next morning Francis hastened back to Assisi, without even seeing Apulia, and, full of quiet joy, he waited for God's further guidance.

Notes on the four plates that follow

17   BATTLING KNIGHTS CARVED ON THE PALAZZO COMUNALE AT
     NARNI
     12th-century relief. Francis' dreams as a young man were filled with the clash of arms.

18   THE DIVINE SPRINGS OF CLITUMNUS
     These springs, with associations of the most primitive cult, lie between Foligno and Spoleto.
     The young Francis rode through this district on his journey in search of knighthood.

19   THE PONTE DELLE TORRI AT SPOLETO
     This bridge is 260 feet high and 650 feet long. It was made out of a Roman aqueduct in
     1362–1370.

20   VIEW OF THE WELL-FORTIFIED TOWN OF SPOLETO

20

The unexpected return of Francis to Assisi led his friends to think that he would resume his gay life of before. He did, indeed, give them a sumptuous banquet, to which a large throng went, singing and shouting through the streets. Francis was leading them as usual, but then he began to become thoughtful and silent. "What's wrong with you?" they asked him, "Have you fallen in love?" Francis turned to them smiling. "Yes," he said, "I have; and she is nobler, richer and lovelier than any other."[10] They laughed at him. But from that day he began to look at things differently. He decided to make a pilgrimage to the tombs of the apostles in Rome, and he hoped there to receive some clear guidance about his future.

At the time the gaze of all Christendom was fixed on Rome, for the great Pope Innocent III was ruling; his remarkable insight and firm government were restoring order in many spheres, both spiritual and temporal. He restored the position of the Papal States, he saved the Church from utter destruction in the East, he negotiated peace between the Christian princes, he aroused among the faithful a deeper sense of their membership of the Church, and with great determination he purged away a number of ecclesiastical abuses which had been embarrassing even the Holy See itself.

It was to this Rome of Innocent III that Francis came as a humble pilgrim. No sooner had he reached the Tomb of St Peter, and seen how poor many of the pilgrims were, than he emptied his purse there and then, and divided his money among them. He then took a beggar aside and exchanged clothes with him; all that day he sat at the door of St Peter's and, speaking in French, begged alms of the passers-by. Thus Francis, clothed in stinking rags and sitting on the ground, experienced for the first time the hunger and the humiliations of poverty. Henceforth he counted himself among the poor, and on his return to Assisi he found growing in his heart an ever greater love of the poor.[11]

He was also beginning to realize daily more deeply the vocation to which Our Lord in His poverty was calling him; to take Lady Poverty as his bride.

Earthly things he began to despise, and to find his only joy in heavenly things. He began to discover that the road of poverty is the royal road to imperishable riches.

Notes on the four plates that follow

21　PILLARS OF THE TEMPLE OF ANTONINUS PIUS AND FAUSTINA IN THE FORUM IN ROME
The ruins of imperial Rome gave Francis pause for thought.

22　THE AQUEDUCT OF THE EMPEROR CLAUDIUS IN THE ROMAN CAMPAGNA

23　THE BRONZE STATUE OF THE APOSTLE IN ST PETER'S
Francis was among the many pilgrims who have kissed the foot of this statue.

24　REMAINS OF THE PALACE OF AUGUSTUS ON THE PALATINE (BEHIND, ON THE RIGHT), WITH THE LOWER PART OF THE PALACE OF SEPTIMUS SEVERUS (IN THE FOREGROUND)
Here probably lived Jacoba di Settesoli, a benefactress of the Saint, whom he called "Brother Jacoba".

24

Francis, the son of the merchant Pietro Bernardone, was growing more and more like the "merchant seeking good pearls, who when he had found one pearl of great price, went his way, and sold all that he had, and bought it".

But he kept his treasure secret, he did not want to risk mockery on its account; so, frequently and even daily, he would retire to the silence of prayer and experience great spiritual sweetness. One day he heard these words: "Francis, you must now learn to despise and hate what you have hitherto loved in the flesh, if you will understand my Will. And once you have begun to do this, you will find that all that was bitter and hard becomes sweet and pleasant, and all that you thought of with terror and gloom will bring you happiness and peace."

Thus his heart was prepared when, riding one day near Assisi, he met a leper. Until now he had always had a feeling of dread of these unfortunate people. But this time he had the strength to overcome his feelings; he got off his horse, handed a gift to the beggar and kissed his hand. And the beggar kissed him.[12] Thenceforward, as he admits in his last will and testament, he found joy in the company of lepers, and in looking after them. For in the sick and the poor he had learnt to recognize Our Lord.

Another day he was praying with special earnestness for God's mercy, and the Lord gave him to understand that he would soon learn what was in store for him. Francis was thereupon filled with consolation.

Shortly after this he was passing the church of San Damiano, and felt somehow compelled to go inside and pray. He went in, and kneeling before the picture of the Crucifix began earnestly to pray. Then a gentle voice came from the Cross: "Francis, don't you see that my house is falling down? Go and build it up again." "Yes, Lord," he answered, "I will." For Francis knew that the little church of San Damiano was crumbling through age.

As he came out of the church, he saw a priest sitting there. He handed him a sum of money. "Please, Father," he said, "would you go and buy some oil with this, and keep a lamp always burning in front of the picture of the Crucifix? If you need any more, I'll get it for you."[13]

After that Francis could never think of the Passion of his Master without weeping.

Notes on the four plates that follow

25   OUTSIDE THE PORTA SAN PIETRO AT ASSISI
It was a beggar like this that first touched the heart of the young Francis.

26   THE CRUCIFIX THAT SPOKE TO ST FRANCIS
The painting was at the time at San Damiano, but is now at Santa Chiara at Assisi.

27   SAN DAMIANO
It was here that Francis asked the priest to keep a lamp burning before the Crucifix.

28   VIEW OVER SAN DAMIANO AND THE PORZIUNCOLA
Amid the olive-trees and cypresses the road leads from Assisi to San Damiano, and then down to Santa Maria degli Angeli in the plain below.

Francis did not hesitate for a moment to carry out the Will of God as he saw it. He loaded his horse with a bale of valuable cloth, and rode down past Spello to Foligno. And there in the market-place, in front of Santa Maria infra Portas, he sold both the cloth and the horse, and brought the proceeds to the poor priest at San Damiano at Assisi. The priest, however, out of fear of the rich Pietro Bernardone's wrath, refused the gift. But he did not refuse the earnest request of Francis, that he should be allowed to stay there with him at San Damiano. Francis was delighted, threw the money down on a window-sill, and thought about it no more.[14]

When Francis did not come home, his father began to organize a search. He felt that his son had changed very much recently, and he summoned various friends and neighbours and proposed to bring him back by force. Francis did not yet feel certain of himself, so he managed to elude the search for more than a month. In the darkness of a cave he prayed, and gradually he received strength and consolation, so that finally he came out and quite openly went to find his father. But the weeks of penance had so changed his appearance that people in the streets laughed at him and threw stones. As he approached the house, with the noisy rabble at his heels, his father heard the noise, came out, leaped upon his son like a wolf on its prey, and locked him up in the house. But Francis thought about the sufferings of his Master, and was able to bear it all with complete patience. When, however, the father was away, his mother came to him and tried in vain to persuade him with gentleness, and eventually set him free. When the father came back, he was, of course, very annoyed, and his next plan was to cite his son before the civil authorities. But Francis would not accept their jurisdiction; he now belonged no more to civilian life, he was a servant of Christ alone. So Bernardone approached Guido, the Bishop of Assisi. Francis was summoned to his presence. "Yes," he said, "I'll go to His Lordship the Bishop, for he is the father and spiritual lord of us all."

In the hall of his palace, next to Santa Maria Maggiore, the bishop solemnly ordered Francis to return the money to his father. "Not only the cash," cried Francis, "you might as well take my clothes too! I will now no longer say, My father Pietro Bernardone, but, Our Father who art in heaven."

The father, partly in anger and partly in sorrow, took the money, gathered up the clothes, and walked out. The naked youth stood there defiantly, until the bishop with a kindly gesture wrapped him round with the edge of his cloak. That was the hour when Francis took Holy Poverty as his bride.[15]

Notes on the four plates that follow

29   AN ALLEY STAIRWAY AT SPELLO
This stairway going up and up without pause, passing through darkness and light, can be seen as a symbol of Francis' life.

30   SAN GRAVIO NEAR SPELLO
Francis rode past this little church on his way to Foligno.

31   THE PILLARED NARTHEX OF SANTA MARIA INFRA PORTAS AT FOLIGNO
This colonnade, built in the 11th or 12th century, was already standing, facing the market-place, when a young man called Francis was selling a bale of cloth there in the year 1205.

32   SANTA MARIA MAGGIORE AT ASSISI, WITH THE ENTRANCE TO THE BISHOP'S PALACE
In a hall within the palace, the episcopal court tried the case between father and son.

32

FRANCIS AT GUBBIO

The bishop continued to cover Francis with his cloak, until one of his servants came up with a shirt and an old tunic. Francis took a piece of brick, and with the white dust chalked a large cross on the tunic. He put it on and set out along the wooded valley of the Tescio. Here he fell among robbers, who asked him who he was. He said: "I am the herald of the great King." The robbers laughed at him, stripped off his tunic, belaboured him, and threw him into a ditch where the snow still lay.[16] Quite unconcerned, Francis struggled out of the snow, and went off to Gubbio, gaily singing the praises of God. Gubbio is an old city, which was already important in Roman times, and Francis sought out a boyhood friend of his who lived there. He needed another tunic now, and he begged a rough working-tunic from his friend. That was in the year 1206.

But the people of Gubbio also treasure another later story about the Saint at Gubbio. On that occasion the whole town was in a panic because of a very fierce wolf, which was a danger not only to animals but also to the people. Francis entered the town, heard about the wolf, and determined to deal with it. The people warned him, but he merely answered that he trusted in God, the master of all creatures. Francis went out to meet the wild wolf, while the people watched anxiously from the walls. They saw the wolf leap at Francis, but suddenly draw back as he made the sign of the Cross. "Come here, Brother Wolf," he said gently, "I command you to do no harm to me or to my friends." The wolf lay down at his feet. "Brother Wolf," Francis went on, "you have been making a lot of trouble round here. You have been mercilessly attacking God's creatures, and even God's own image in man, and everyone is quite rightly complaining. But I want you to be at peace with the town, and I promise you that as long as you live the people of this town will feed you every day, but only provided you promise never again to harm man or beast." The wolf bowed its head, and put its paw into Francis' hand. It did this again afterwards in the public market-place, and all the people solemnly promised to look after the wolf. They then cried out, praising God, and thanking him

[17]

for sending Francis, by whose merits the wolf had been tamed and become as gentle as a lamb.

Thenceforward the wolf lived quietly in the city, and every day went from door to door and was befriended by everybody. When two years later the wolf died, all the town mourned, for the creature had been to them a constant reminder of the holiness of Francis.[17]

Notes on the four plates that follow

33 THE NARROW VALLEY OF THE TESCIO NEAR ASSISI
It was about here that Francis was attacked by robbers.

34 A ROMAN GATEWAY AT GUBBIO
At Gubbio Francis got from a friend the rough garment which was a symbol of his penance.

35 GUBBIO, WITH MONTE INGINO BEHIND
In the foreground are the remains of the Roman amphitheatre.

36 THE SAINT'S HABIT
This garment is preserved at Santa Chiara at Assisi. It is a habit of the pattern later worn by St Francis and his brethren. The tunic which he got at Gubbio was more like a pilgrim's tunic, with a belt, wallet and staff.

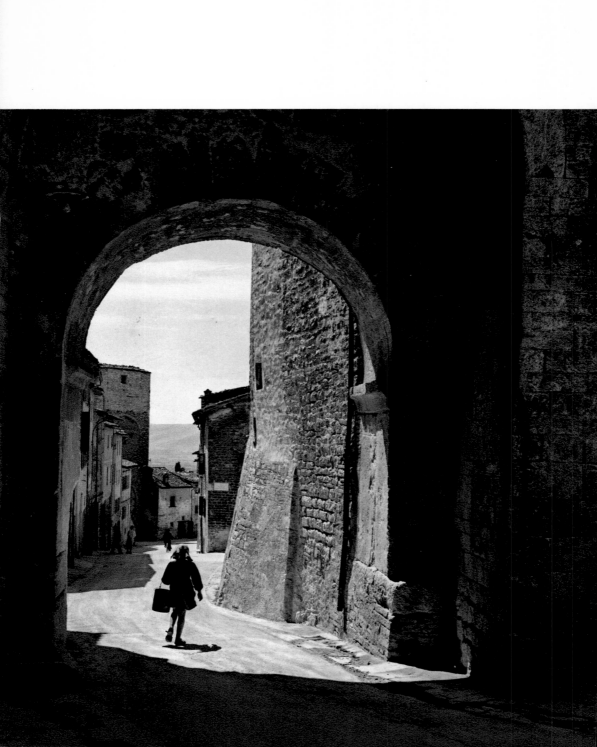

36

FRANCIS THE CHURCH-BUILDER

Francis had not forgotten the words he heard from the Crucifix at San Damiano. So often on his wanderings he had visited sanctuaries, built long ago as a gesture of piety, and now, in an age when piety had cooled, falling into neglect. Francis then began to go through the streets, singing and begging for building-stones. "Whoever gives me a stone, will get a reward in heaven; whoever gives me two, will get a double reward; three stones will bring a reward three times over!"[18] Many people laughed at him, but others were touched by his simplicity, and he collected very many stones, which he then carried to San Damiano on his own shoulders. There he worked, and gradually rebuilt the crumbling walls, singing French songs as he worked. At first the custodian of the sanctuary gave him his meals, but then he began to slip away at mealtimes and beg his food from door to door. At first he felt disgusted as he attempted to swallow the scraps and oddments that people gave him, but gradually he overcame this and was able to do so easily and gaily.[19] When he had restored San Damiano to its original beauty, he turned his attention to the church of St Peter outside the city, and then with special zeal he tackled Santa Maria Maggiore and Santa Maria degli Angeli, which was known to the people as the Porziuncola.

During this time he occasionally met his father. And every time his father cursed him. So Francis used to take round with him an old beggar, whom he instructed to bless him whenever his father cursed him. "Look," said Francis to Pietro Bernardone, "God has given me an old father to bless me every time you curse me."[20]

Notes on the four plates that follow

37 SAN DAMIANO AT ASSISI
The first church to be restored by Francis.

38 THE PORZIUNCOLA
Little did he know, as he worked to rebuild these walls, what a beloved and holy place this
was to be to him later on.

39 SANTA MARIA MAGGIORE
This view includes (from left to right) the bishop's palace, Santa Maria Maggiore (also called
Santa Maria del Vescovado), the tower of the Town Hall, and above, the fortress called the
Rocca Maggiore.

40 ROMANESQUE APSE OF SANTA MARIA MAGGIORE
The Saint worked much at the restoration of this church. There is a stone in the wall of the
apse, with an inscription which perhaps refers to his labours: "1216 . . . in the tenth year, in the
time of Bishop Guido and of Brother Francis."

40

One day—it was the feast of St Matthias, February 24th 1209—Francis was at Mass and heard the priest reading from the Gospel words from the tenth chapter of St Matthew, which made a great impression on him: "Do not possess gold, nor silver, nor money in your purses, nor scrip for your journey, nor two coats, nor shoes, nor a staff." He asked the priest to explain the passage to him, and then he joyfully exclaimed: "That's what I'm going to do." Immediately he abandoned everything but the strictest necessities.[21]

The holiness of his life now became apparent to all, and before long a few men were seized with his spirit of penance and began to follow him in his way of life and to wear the same kind of clothes. The first of these was Brother Bernard of Quintavalle, a man of Assisi. Shortly afterwards, Brother Peter of Cattaneo joined them. These three went one morning into the church of St Nicholas, in the centre of the town. There they prayed earnestly, and, in honour of the Holy Trinity, opened three times the Book of the Gospels, to seek therein the will of God. The first time they read: "If thou wilt be perfect, go, sell what thou hast, and give to the poor, and thou shalt have treasure in heaven." At the second opening: "And he commanded them that they should take nothing for the way." And the third time: "If any man will come after me, let him deny himself." Then Francis turned to his companions: "That," he said, "will be our Rule, and the way of life for all who come with us; now, Brethren, let us go and do what we have been told." The three men came out of the church. Bernard, who was a very rich man, went off and sold his house and all his property and distributed the proceeds to the poor of the town. Another early companion, a holy man and one of Francis' most trusted friends, Egidio or Giles of Assisi, did likewise.[22] Soon the company numbered twelve, and among them was a knight, Angelo Tancredi of Rieti, whose house was later to become the home of the spiritual daughters of St Francis.

Notes on the four plates that follow

41   CRYPT OF THE PARISH CHURCH OF ST NICHOLAS AT ASSISI
      It was here that Francis opened the Book of the Gospels, to seek therein the will of God.

42   THE HOUSE OF THE RICH MAN BERNARD OF QUINTAVALLE
      (far centre, with the round-arched doorway)
      Francis had been invited to stay with Bernard in this house, and here Bernard watched him
      at prayer during the night. This sight moved Bernard to throw in his lot with Francis.

43   THE HOUSE OF BERNARD OF QUINTAVALLE
      (right foreground)

44   THE HOUSE OF THE KNIGHT ANGELO TANCREDI, AT RIETI
      Angelo was the twelfth companion, who joined after Francis had said to him: "You have had
      enough of weapons and war; come with me, and I'll make you a knight of Christ."

44

THEY CHOOSE TO BE HOMELESS

"The foxes have holes, and the birds of the air nests; but the son of man hath not where to lay his head" (Matt. 8. 20). Francis and his first brethren wished to be no richer than Our Lord in His poverty. They therefore never entered any of the houses in the town, except as Christ's messengers of peace or as beggars. Instead, they sought caves or shacks in the fields outside the city, and there, hidden from men's gaze, they devoted themselves to prayer and penance.

Whenever the holy man left his solitude and met people on the road, he always talked with them, and urged them to love God, to fear Him, and to do penance for their sins.[23] For the love of God was at that time little esteemed, and it seemed as if the temptations of the flesh, the wiles of the world, and the pride of life had so laid hands on the world, that it seemed to be rushing to its ruin. Many people, indeed, were touched by God's grace when they met the brethren, but there were few of these who had the courage to throw in their lot with them. Francis said to Brother Giles: "Our Order is like a trawler, who throws his net into the sea and gathers an enormous number of fish; the little ones he throws back into the water, but the big ones he keeps." How true this was, was shown later, when men and women with big and generous hearts were received into the Order, while those with small minds and faint hearts were rejected.

Notes on the four plates that follow

45 A STRAW SHACK IN THE VALE OF RIETI
The shepherds still today build themselves shacks like this one, as a shelter against storms.
It was probably in shacks of this kind that the first brethren took refuge.

46 THE INSIDE OF A CAVE NEAR THE CARCERI IN THE DISTRICT
OF ASSISI
Each brother lived alone in a cave.

47 ANOTHER CAVE NEAR THE CARCERI
O beata solitudo, o sola beatitudo—O blessed solitude, o sole beatitude!

48 A THIRD CAVE IN THE RAVINE OF THE CARCERI
"O all ye things that spring up in the earth, bless the Lord: praise him and exalt him above all
for ever."

[24]

48

RIVOTORTO

It was not long before the first brethren desired to live in community with Francis, in order to keep his living example all the time before them. So in 1209 these lovers of holy poverty settled down all together in some ruined hovels called Rivotorto near Assisi, on the banks of a winding stream. There was so little space that Francis wrote up the name of each brother above his place. They would pray in common before a big wooden cross, which they had put up in front of the hovels.

The brethren lived in the greatest poverty at Rivotorto, but they led a life of still greater holiness and charity. Their company was growing, and it was becoming necessary to give it a formal status. At this stage, therefore, Francis wrote his first Rule, according to which in a very few and simple words he bound his brethren to a life of poverty and holiness in the spirit of the Gospel. Francis and his brethren next went off to Rome to seek papal approbation of the Rule. Pope Innocent III received them very kindly, but refused to grant approbation to the Rule, which he felt to be altogether too strict.[24] But, after this, Innocent had a dream, in which he saw the Lateran Basilica falling down and Francis with his own strength holding it up. The next day the Pope received him again, embraced him, blessed him, and gave him and his brethren permission to preach and to live according to the new Rule. Francis and his brethren then returned to their beloved Rivotorto.[25]

Shortly afterwards a certain farmer came and insisted on stabling his donkey in the miserable shelters of the brethren. The man was very rude to them, and Francis, preferring to avoid strife, decided it would be better to leave Rivotorto altogether.[26]

Notes on the our plates that follow

49   THE TUGURIUM

The hovels in which Francis and the twelve brethren lived were reconstructed in 1929 in the modern gothic church at Rivotorto.

50
51   THE HOLY PLACES OF ASSISI

To the right is the town of Assisi itself, and in the plain below lie the Porziuncola in the centre and Rivotorto to the left.

52   A DONKEY-DRIVER FROM THE NEIGHBOURHOOD OF ASSISI

[26]

49

50 >
51 >

52

MONTE SUBASIO

When Francis and his brethren were driven out of Rivotorto, the saint said to the others: "I think it would be a good and holy thing if we were to ask the bishop, or the canons of San Rufino, or the abbot of the Benedictines on Monte Subasio, for a church where the brethren could recite the Divine Office. We should then want only a quite small and simple sort of mud hut, in which to sleep and work." So he went to the Bishop of Assisi and asked him. "I'm sorry," said the bishop, "I have no church I could give you." And the canons said the same. So he went to the Abbot of Monte Subasio. The abbot was full of sympathy and, after asking the advice of his monks, decided to give the brethren the sanctuary known as Santa Maria di Porziuncola or Santa Maria degli Angeli, which was a small and humble little church. "We have agreed", said the abbot, "to let you have this chapel; and if with God's help your Order should grow large, we would like you to look upon this place as the centre of the whole Order." Francis accepted the chapel with many thanks, but he did not look upon it as their possession, for this, he felt, would have offended perfect poverty; he regarded the chapel as lent to them by the monks, and he therefore used every year to send to the abbot and the monks a basket of fish—it was a freshwater fish called a *lasca*—as a kind of rent. But every time the abbot sent in return a vessel of oil.[27] Thus it was, in fact, a gift of St Benedict, the father of Western monasticism, to St Francis, who was to put new life into the observance of the evangelical counsels; it was the Benedictines who provided the Franciscans with their first roof over their heads and their first altar of their own.

Nearby the brethren built huts of twigs and mud, or else bowers of leafy branches; they slept on sacks filled with straw, and the bare earth served as seats and table; a simple hedge served as a wall round the encampment. The brethren begged for bread from door to door, trying to imitate the poverty of Christ. They worked chiefly in the leper-hospital, or else helped the farmers, working in the fields. They would never accept money for their work, for this was to them a symbol of the world, which for Christ's sake they had left behind. Francis once said it had been revealed to him that, since God had given him so many graces at the Porziuncola, this chapel was more loved by Our Lady than any other of her churches throughout the world.[28]

Notes on the four plates that follow

53   THE CRYPT OF THE BENEDICTINE CHURCH ON MONTE SUBASIO
The romanesque vault makes a fine pattern over the altar.

54   THE RUINS OF THE ABBEY OF MONTE SUBASIO
Here Francis came with his request to the kindly abbot, who gave him the Porziuncola.

55   VIEW FROM MONTE SUBASIO OVER ASSISI TOWARDS PERUGIA

56   ANOTHER PHOTOGRAPH OF THE CRYPT AT MONTE SUBASIO
Still today one can sense a holiness about this place, sanctified by the presence of St Francis.

THE PORZIUNCOLA

The sanctuary of the Porziuncola, the gift to Francis from the Abbot of Monte Subasio, had already for centuries been regarded as a holy place by the local population. Angels, it was said, had frequently appeared here; and it was here that Francis received God's call to follow a life of poverty.

He specially loved the dense forest of oaks that extended all the way from the Porziuncola up to the city itself. In this forest he and his brethren were able, unseen by men, to give themselves to ardent prayer, and together with their sisters the birds in the trees to sing the praises of God's goodness. Here they spent together the first glad springtime of their new vocation, and never were devotion and poverty practised with such simple zeal as here.

One of the brethren, before his conversion, had an ecstasy, and in the ecstasy he saw the little chapel of the Porziuncola surrounded by a huge crowd of people, all kneeling with their faces upturned to heaven. And then he realized that every one of these people was blind. Suddenly there came out of heaven a dazzling light, and blindness of all eyes and hearts was instantly healed.

This brother's vision was fulfilled in an unexpected way. It was a summer night in 1216, and Francis was praying. During his prayer God told him to go to the Pope and ask of him the following favour: that whoever with a contrite heart and after sacramental confession should visit the Porziuncola chapel would be delivered from all temporal punishment. Next morning Francis was away to Perugia with Brother Masseo, to visit the recently elected Pope Honorius III and to place his request before him. The Pope hesitated to grant it, for he was anxious not to compromise any of the indulgences attached to the crusades. But Francis soon disposed of his doubts: "My Lord," he said, "the request is not mine, but of Him who sent me, Jesus Christ himself." The Pope thereupon granted the indulgence, to be obtained on the day of the dedication of the chapel, the feast of St Peter's Chains, and on that day every year. Francis had hoped to get the indulgence for eight days, but decided to be content with what he had achieved. He turned to leave, but the Pope called after him: "Here, you simpleton, where are you going? How will you prove that you have had the indulgence granted?" "Your word is good enough for me," replied Francis, "I don't want any papers: Our Lady is the document, Christ has signed it, and the angels are the witnesses." At the ceremony of dedication, attended by seven bishops, Francis mounted a wooden pulpit in front of the chapel and announced the indulgence: "What I want above all," he said, "is that you should all get to heaven. I am therefore announcing to you an indulgence, which I myself got for you from the lips of my Lord the Pope; whoever is here today, and whoever comes any year on this day to this chapel with a truly contrite heart, gains an indulgence remitting all punishment due to his sins."

After this he left in God's hands any further publication of this favour, knowing full well that He would do all that was necessary.

And, in fact, the numbers grew greater every year of those who came, both to receive the indulgence and to breathe the fresh atmosphere of those early days of the Franciscan spirit. Thus it was that the little chapel of the Porziuncola, later enclosed in an enormous basilica, came to be one of the principal places of pilgrimage in the world.

Notes on the four plates that follow

57 THE WOOD NEAR THE FRIARY OF THE FRIARS MINOR AT SANTA MARIA DEGLI ANGELI
This wood reminds us of the oak-forest which used to surround the Porziuncola.

58 THE ENTRANCE TO THE CHAPEL
Hic locus sanctus est—This is a holy place!

59 INTERIOR OF THE CHAPEL

60 AMID THE TREES
Francis and his first brethren built their huts amid the trees: the forest was their friary, and the little chapel in the woods was their first church.

57 ▷

58 ▷
59 ▷

THE CARCERI

In the side of the hill above the Porziuncola there is a series of caves in the limestone. These caves are known as the Carceri, that is, the "prisons", and they were a favourite refuge for Francis and his brethren when they wanted to be alone with God. One day Francis was returning from that wooded solitude to the Porziuncola, and at the edge of the wood he met Brother Masseo. Now Brother Masseo wanted to put the Saint's humility to the test. "Why always you?" he cried. "Why always you?" Francis then said quietly: "And what is Brother Masseo talking about?" Brother Masseo said: "Why is it that everyone runs after you all the time, and wants to follow you? Why always you? You are nothing to look at; you are not particularly clever; you are not even well-born. Why is it always you?" Francis was delighted and greatly moved. He stood there silent for a while, looking up to the sky. Then he threw himself to his knees to praise God and to thank him. "You want to know," he cried passionately to Brother Masseo, "you want to know why it's always me? Well, listen to this: when God looked down on all the bad men of the earth, he could not find a greater sinner than me, the worst and meanest of all; but he had a great work that needed doing, and since he could find no poorer creature than me to do it, he chose me. For 'the foolish things of the world hath God chosen, that he may confound the wise; and the weak things of the world hath God chosen, that he may confound the strong.' " Brother Masseo felt overwhelmed by such passionate humility, and he now knew for certain that this was a true disciple of Christ.[29]

Among the brethren was Brother Juniper, who was specially beloved of Francis because of his utter simplicity. Francis used to say: "I wish I had a whole forest of junipers!" Brother Juniper always carried out Francis' instructions to the letter, so that on his example he would never turn away a poor man as long as he had anything to give him. He had to be stopped giving away the clothes off his own back; but he then suggested to a beggar that he should pull them off him by force, to which the brother then offered no serious resistance. Francis himself one day gave to a poor woman the only copy of the Gospels they had at the Porziuncola, because he could not find anything else to give her; for he thought it was more important to observe the spirit of the Gospel than to possess the letter.

Notes on the four plates that follow

61   THE TWO CHAPELS OF THE CARCERI
The further chapel belongs to the time of St Francis, but the friary is of later construction.

62   THE COURT OF THE HILLSIDE FRIARY OF THE CARCERI

63   A NUT-TREE BELOW THE FRIARY
It was on the trees in the background that the birds were sitting when St Francis preached to them.

64   A STAIRCASE IN THE FRIARY
The handrail of unplaned wood is a symbol of the spirit of poverty, still today so alive at the Carceri.

64

SAINT CLARE

Salvation came to the world through a Woman, and so among God's servants there have always been women. And among the friends of St Francis, servants of God, there was also a wonderful woman. She lived at Assisi in a grand house, being the daughter of Faverone dei Scifi and his wife Ortolana Fiumi. Her name was Clare, and before long the light of her holiness was to shine throughout the world.

It was during a sermon of Francis that she realized that her vocation lay in the service of God in poverty. Francis heard about her, and resolved forthwith to rob the world of this treasure, and so to enrich Christ his own Master. On a certain Palm Sunday Clare was at Mass, adorned with all her finery, and received from the hand of Bishop Guido the blest olive-branch.

That night she slipped away secretly from her father's house, and went to the Porziuncola, where she received the habit of penance and vowed obedience to Francis. Next morning Francis took her to the Benedicfine nuns at Sant' Angelo in Panzo, near Assisi.

When, however, her younger sister Agnes went there to join her, the family took drastic measures to fetch the younger girl back, but they failed.

Francis then decided to gather his spiritual daughters in one place, so as to be able to form them in the spirit of his Rule, and he asked the Bishop of Assisi for the little church of San Damiano, which the bishop most willingly gave him for this purpose. Clare then moved to San Damiano, where for forty-one years "the alabaster box of her body was broken by the violence of her penance, so that the whole Church was filled with the fragrance of her life".

San Damiano became the centre of a new life of prayer, poverty, and joy, and Clare struggled fearlessly to defend the right to live in poverty as Our Lord had done.

Notes on the four plates that follow

65   THE NUNS' CHOIR AT SAN DAMIANO

66   A CORNER OF THE CHAPEL, SHOWING THE STAIRS TO THE
DORMITORY

67   THE REFECTORY
Here we see so plainly the loveliness of Franciscan poverty.

68   THE HAIR OF ST CLARE
The precious relic is preserved at the Convent of St Clare at Assisi. She cut off her hair when
she first went to the Porziuncola to offer her life to God.

67

68

THE FIRST FOUNDATIONS

As the number of the brethren increased, the influence of St Francis began to spread, first through Umbria and then gradually through other parts of Italy. And the places where Francis was at first inhospitably received were before long echoing to his message of the love of God and penance. The following is a list of the places visited by St Francis and the brethren, sanctified by their presence, and chosen for the early foundations. Each one of these names has become renowned in Franciscan history.

The Porziuncola   the most beloved of all by Francis;

Rivotorto   where he wrote the first Rule;

The Carceri   where the oratory dates from the time of Francis, though the friary was founded by St Bernardine of Siena;

Monte Casale   where Francis entertained some robbers, and received them as brothers;

Baschi   where he preached to the fishes;

Bologna   the site of the small friary, to which in 1219 a house of studies was attached, to the displeasure of the Saint;

Poggio Bustone   where Francis received the assurance that the sins of his youth were forgiven;

La Verna   the mountain of the five wounds;

Monte Rainerio   now known as *Fonte Colombo*, where the new Rule of the Order was composed;

Sarteano   where the Devil pursued Francis;

Greccio   where Francis officiated as deacon at Christmas;

Cetona   a foundation made by Francis as he preached penance in the neighbourhood;

Celle di Cortona   a favourite halting-place of the Saint;

La Foresta   where Francis by a miracle multiplied the produce of a vineyard that had been robbed;

Venice	where Francis came ashore, on an island in the lagoon, when he returned from his journey to the East;
Todi	where he founded a home for abandoned children;
Florence	where Brother Bernard and Brother Giles stopped on their way to Spain, and slept out of doors on a cold night; and were afterwards hospitably entertained on account of their holiness.

And so the foundations multiplied, so that soon the whole world was hearing the preaching of St Francis and his sons.

Notes on the eight plates that follow

69   A SMALL WOOD NEAR THE FRIARY AT CELLE DI CORTONA

70   THE PRESENT CAPUCHIN FRIARY AT CELLE DI CORTONA

71   THE CELL OF ST FRANCIS AT CELLE DI CORTONA
The Saint's poverty is still the rich treasure of this place.

72
73   UMBRIAN LANDSCAPE
View towards Chiusi and Arezzo from the height of the two foundations at Sarteano and Cetona.

74   OUR LADY OF MONTE CASALE
This statue was given to Francis by a certain nobleman. The precious jewellery that now adorns it has small value compared to the fact that Francis prayed before it.

75   THE CELL OF ST FRANCIS AT MONTE CASALE
The stone at the top right of the photograph is supposed to be where he slept.

76   THE FRIARY GARDEN AT MONTE CASALE
The Capuchins of Monte Casale still plant every year a cabbage in their garden, and let it flower. This is the cabbage in the photograph. For it was here that Francis, to test the obedience of two of the brethren, ordered them to plant some young cabbage plants upside down. One of them failed the test and, contradicting the command, planted them in the usual way: and he was dismissed from the Order. The cabbage in the garden today still commemorates the occurrence.

[36]

69

70   71

72
73

SAINT FRANCIS AND THE ANIMALS

Since God's goodness extends to all creatures, Francis extended his mercy and affection not only to all mankind, but also to irrational creatures. And he quite specially loved animals.

While he was at the Porziuncola someone gave him a lamb, to which he was greatly attached, not only because of the creature's simplicity, but also because it put them all in mind of the Lamb of God. He told the lamb that it must not disturb the brethren at their prayers, and so, whenever they came into choir, the lamb used to come into the church and, without ever having been taught to do so, used to kneel down most devoutly. It also used to go to the Lady Altar and bleat there before her statue as if in greeting.

Another time Francis and another brother were in the Venetian lagoon and came across a lot of birds singing in the rushes. Francis said: "Our sisters the birds are singing God's praises; let us sing our Office with them." But the two brethren soon found that they could not hear each other for the sound of the bird-song. "My sisters," said Francis, turning to the little birds, "you just stop singing until we have finished our Office." Whereupon they all remained silent until the end; then Francis told them to start again, and instantly the air was filled with their song.

A young man of Siena had caught many doves in a trap, and was taking them alive to market. Francis met him on the road. "My good young man," he said, "please give me those doves. These innocent creatures are likened in the Scriptures to pure souls, full of faith and humility; they ought not to fall into cruel hands that kill them." The young man gave him the doves at once. Francis took them in his arms, and spoke to them gently: "My little sisters, innocent doves, why do you let yourselves be caught like that? I will look after you and build nests for you, and if God wills, you will have little ones." And he did build nests for them, and they became so tame that they never flew away from the brethren until Francis had given them a blessing. And as for the young man, Francis told him that he would join the Order and become a true servant of God, which, in fact, did come to pass, and he lived an exemplary life until his death.

Francis was once walking along the road from Cannara to Bevagna. There were flocks of birds in the trees by the roadside and more of them scattered about the fields. Francis said to his companions: "Wait here on the road, until I come back: I want to go over there and preach to my sisters the birds." He had scarcely begun to preach than all the birds in the trees flew down and remained motionless on the ground, while he walked about among them, even brushing them with the hem of his habit, and not one of them flew away. And this is what he said to them: "My little sisters, you have a lot to thank God for, and you must never forget to praise him. You are free to fly where you like, you have got plenty of clothing, you have gaily coloured habits, you get your food without difficulty, you sing lovely songs which are also a gift of God. And look at the crowd of you: God gives you large families. He even took care of you in the Ark. The air is all your own. You don't have to sow or reap, and God looks after you. There are streams and springs for you to drink from, mountains and hills, high rocks and cliffs for your refuge, tall trees for you to nest in. So you must love your Creator who is so good to you; and, my little sisters, take care never to be ungrateful to him, but spend your lives in praising him."

Thereupon the birds began to open their beaks and spread their wings, they stretched out their necks and bowed their heads, and with all kinds of noises and gestures showed how delighted they were with what he had said. Francis was so happy, praised God, and invited them all to join in the praise. Then he made a great sign of the Cross over them all and sent them away; they all flew up into the sky with a great song, and Francis blessed them again with the sign of the Cross. They then divided into four groups, flying away to the four points of the compass. This was a sign that the brethren should preach the Cross to the four quarters of the earth, and, like the birds, should possess nothing, but trust entirely to God's providence.[30]

When Francis was staying near Greccio, a hare was caught in a snare, and someone brought it alive to him. He felt sorry for the creature, and said to it:

"Little brother hare, come here. Why are you so stupid about snares?" And he let the hare go, whereupon it hopped into his lap, and he held it there, stroking it gently. He then put it down, for it to run away into the wood, but each time he put it down it always came back to him. Finally, he had to tell some of the brethren to carry it away and put it down inside the wood.

A nobleman of Siena once gave a pheasant to Francis when he was ill. Francis received the pheasant gladly, and said to it: "Brother pheasant, let us praise our Creator!" To the brethren he said: "Let us see whether Brother pheasant will stay with us, or whether he would rather go back to his usual hiding-place." So he told one of the brethren to carry the bird away to a certain vineyard. But the pheasant immediately flew back to Francis. They tried again, carrying it farther away, but again the pheasant flew back and crouched among the brethren in their little hut. Francis fed and caressed it. But then a friend of theirs, who was a doctor, begged them to let him have the creature, and kept it in his house. But at the doctor's house the bird would not touch any food, so that he brought it back to Francis. As soon as the creature saw Francis again, it cheered up, and at once returned to its food.

Notes on the four plates that follow

77 SHEEP IN THE VALE OF RIETI

Sheep and lambs were the favourite animals of St Francis, because they reminded him of the Lamb of God.

78 DOVES AT ASSISI

These doves are in the narthex of the church of Santa Maria sopra Minerva at Assisi. The pillars belonged to the ancient temple. Doves were for Francis symbols of innocence.

79 SWALLOWS IN THE GARDEN OF THE FRIARY AT SAN DAMIANO

80 BROTHER ASS

When Francis was ill and the wounds on his feet made it difficult for him to walk, it was Brother Ass who carried him along the roads of Umbria.

78 >
79 >

FARMER JOHN JOINS ST FRANCIS

A great characteristic of St Francis was his simplicity, and he loved to see true simplicity in his brethren.

As he went about preaching, he was often pained to notice how dusty and dirty some churches were. He would then approach the priest in charge of them, and ask him quite humbly to keep the church cleaner out of reverence to God. Often he would set to with a broom himself.

Once he entered a chapel which was sadly neglected and he immediately began to sweep it. A farmer named John, who at the time was ploughing in a field nearby, hastened to the chapel and asked Francis if he might be allowed to help him. So they worked together, and when they had cleaned the whole chapel, John turned to St Francis. "Brother," he said, "for a long time I have wanted to come and serve God together with you and the brethren, but I didn't know how to get in touch with you. Now God has arranged it, and I am ready to do whatever you tell me."

Francis was delighted and explained to him that if he wanted to join them, he must sell his property and give the proceeds to the poor, as it says in the Gospel: "If thou wilt be perfect, go, sell what thou hast, and give to the poor."

John thereupon went back to his oxen in the field, unyoked the animals, and brought one of them to Francis, saying: "Brother Francis, my inheritance is small enough, because I have always worked in my own family; but I am claiming this ox as my share, and I am giving it to the poor." But when his parents heard what he was going to do, they came along with his younger brothers and made a great fuss. They seemed to be more distressed about the loss of the animal than about the young man's departure. Francis, however, gave them a meal and consoled them, saying: "I can't give you back your brother, because he belongs to God; but since you are poor, I am ordering him to give up the ox and give it back to you." The young man did so, and was then clothed in the habit of penance.

Brother John was so simple that he thought he should imitate whatever he saw Francis doing. When Francis was praying, John imitated every movement: when Francis knelt down, he knelt down; when Francis raised his hands, he raised his hands, and so forth. He even imitated his way of sighing or coughing. When Francis eventually noticed this, he scolded John but in a very kindly way, because he was amused by his simplicity. John lived only a short time, but even in that short time he acquired a reputation for sanctity.

Later on, Francis often used to tell the story of John, though he did not speak of him as "Brother John", but always as "the holy John".[31]

Notes on the four plates that follow

81   A FARMER PLOUGHING NEAR ASSISI

82   A FARMER ON HIS WAY HOME NEAR ARMENZANO
This is the village where Farmer John joined St Francis.

83   THE STEEP SLOPES OF ARMENZANO
At the bottom right of the photograph a man is ploughing with a pair of white oxen.

84   A FINE YOKE OF OXEN

84

On July 16th 1212, the Spanish army won a glorious victory over the Moors at Las Navas, and the whole Christian world expected soon to see the reconquest of the Holy Land. The general enthusiasm caught also the chivalrous spirit of Francis, but, much as he loved the places hallowed by Our Lord's presence, he was not thinking in terms of mere conquest of the land, but rather of the capture of the souls of the infidels for Christ.

He therefore set off with some of the brethren for the harbour city of Ancona. They will certainly have visited Our Lady's sanctuary there, recently completed, Santa Maria della Piazza, to ask the Star of the Sea to look after them. The venerable features of this church still greet the traveller as he approaches the quay.

Eventually they set sail, but they had scarcely reached the open sea, when a fierce storm drove the vessel on to the coast of Dalmatia. It was impossible to resume the voyage, and only after the greatest difficulties did the travellers regain the Italian coast at Ancona.[32]

A little way south of Ancona there is a small town called Osimo. Near here they met a man tending some goats, and among the goats was a solitary little lamb quietly grazing. Francis was greatly touched by the scene: "That little lamb", he said with a sigh, "is like Our Blessed Lord among the Pharisees: for the love of him let us buy the lamb, and get it out of the company of the goats!" Brother Paul agreed, though they had nothing with them but their rough habits and did not know what to do about paying for it. At that moment a merchant came along and offered to buy the lamb for them. The brethren accepted it gratefully and took it with them into Osimo. There they called on the bishop, who received them with much courtesy, but was a little astonished about the lamb that Francis brought with him and seemed greatly attached to. Francis, however, uttered so lovely a discourse about the lamb's likeness to Our Lord, that the bishop was greatly impressed. The next day they presented the lamb to the nuns of San Severino, who received it gladly, and later on

[43]

made from its wool a habit, which they sent to St Francis at the time of the General Chapter at the Porziuncola. The holy man received the gift with reverence and joy, kissed it and invited the others to share his happiness.[33]

Notes on the four plates that follow

85   THE VIEW FROM OSIMO TOWARDS ANCONA

This view is taken from the bishop's palace in Old Osimo, and extends across the fertile fields to the heights above Ancona.

86
87   FISHING VESSELS IN THE HARBOUR OF ANCONA

It was here that Francis' voyage began and ended.

88   SANTA MARIA DELLA PIAZZA AT ANCONA

The church was completed in 1210. Here Francis and his companions sought the protection of Our Lady before the voyage.

[44]

86

SOME TYPICAL STORIES

At one time, when Francis withdrew into a remote place to devote himself in solitude to prayer and penance, he made friends there with a falcon. Whenever Francis intended to rise during the night to pray, the falcon used to wake him up at the right time with its cries. When, however, Francis was ill, the falcon took care not to call him at night, but waited until the morning to rouse him.[34]

A certain fisherman once caught a large fish in the lake of Piediluco, and presented it to Francis. Francis accepted it politely, but then began to talk to the fish and to address it as a brother. He then carefully put it back into the water and began to pray aloud. As long as the prayer continued, the fish would not leave the side of the boat in which the Saint was sitting. But when the prayer was ended, and Francis gave the fish leave, it swam gaily away.[35]

One day Francis was riding on a donkey which a peasant had lent him. It was very hot and the path was very steep. The peasant, who was lagging behind, called out to Francis that he was dying of thirst and that Francis must help him. Francis got off the donkey, raised his hands to heaven and asked for God's assistance. Then he said to the peasant: "Now hurry up; on the top there you'll find water: Our Lord has put it there splashing over the rocks, specially for you." And there, where in spite of careful searching water was never known before or after, the peasant was able fully to quench his thirst.[36]

The small town of Baschi has two special memories of St Francis. One concerns the three sons of Count Ugolino who were engaged in a violent quarrel and were about to take up arms when Francis stepped in between them and settled the matter. The brothers were so grateful that they built him a small friary there. The other story recounts how he preached to the fishes in the River Tiber which flows past the town. The people still point out the stone from which he preached.[37]

In the autumn of 1217 Francis arrived at Arezzo, where the citizens were divided into two factions. As he lay on the first night in the poor-house, he heard noisy shouting and the clash of arms outside. Next morning he sent his companion, Brother Silvester, to stand in the city-gate and to utter an exorcism, commanding all evil spirits in the name of God to leave the city forthwith. Brother Silvester went as he was told, and stood up and shouted: "All devils get out of here! I'm saying this in the name of Almighty God and by order of his servant Francis." The factions very soon afterwards made peace, and the agreement drawn up on December 31st 1217 remained ever afterwards in force.

But the greatest gift that Francis received from Arezzo was a gift to the whole Order. The noble lord, Stephen (apparently from the family of the Nerbotto Sterpoli), offered a house for a Franciscan foundation, and many distinguished citizens entered the Order there. Two important names in 13th-century Franciscan history are those of Benedict Sinigardi and Angelo Tarlati, both of whom belonged to the Arezzo community.[38]

Notes on the four plates that follow

89 A CHAPEL BETWEEN BETTONA AND SANTA MARIA DEGLI ANGELI
This chapel was erected to mark the spot where a spring of water appeared at the command of Francis.

90 THE LAKE OF PIEDILUCO
Here Francis was given a fish, which he put back into the water, and which would not leave him until he told it to do so.

91 THE TIBER NEAR BASCHI
From this stone it is said that Francis preached to the fishes.

92 THE CHURCH OF PIEVE DI SANTA MARIA AT AREZZO
Arezzo was the city which Brother Silvester, on the orders of Francis, delivered from evil spirits which caused internal strife. The fine façade of this church was completed during the lifetime of St Francis.

92

THE GIFT OF LA VERNA

The lord of the little town of San Leo was celebrating a great festival, in the course of which he was going to receive his knighthood. Among the guests was a certain Count Orlando Catanio, lord of Chiusi Nuovo and owner of the mountain known as La Verna. Francis, who had been preaching nearby, went into the feast. They had begun with a religious service, and after this Francis addressed the merry gathering. He began with these words:

> Tanto è il ben ch'aspetto,
> Ch'ogni pena m'è diletto.

> So great the heavenly joy I see,
> That earthly pain is sweet to me.

Orlando afterwards went up to Francis. "Brother Francis," he said, "there is a mountain in Tuscany called La Verna, in a remote and lonely spot. It belongs to me. If you and your brethren would like to have it, I would love to give it to you."

Francis thanked God and Count Orlando. He told him to stay on at the feast, but when Count Orlando had returned home, Francis sent two of the brethren to him. He received them with as much honour as if angels had visited him, and instantly set out with them for La Verna. He took with him a company of fifty men, for defence against wild beasts, and when they reached the top, they built a few cells there for the brethren. The two brethren then returned to Francis and reported that it was a very lonely place and most conducive to contemplation.

Once more Francis thanked God and praised his goodness to them.

Notes on the four plates that follow

93   THE HILL-TOWN OF SAN LEO
The road on the left leads up to the town, where Francis met Count Orlando.

94   VIEW OF THE TOWN AND ITS CASTLE
The church and castle face each other on the hill-top.

95   THE ROMANESQUE CHURCH OF SAN LEO
It was in the market-place in front of the church, on May 8th 1213, that Francis addressed the festive gathering and afterwards received the gift of La Verna.

96   VIEW FROM THE PASSO DELLA CONSUMA TOWARDS THE VALE
OF BIBBIENA
In the distance, to the left, wrapped in cloud, is La Verna.

[48]

96

St Francis used to summon the brethren twice a year for a general chapter. At one of these gatherings at Santa Maria degli Angeli there were about five thousand brethren present. On one occasion it is believed that St Dominic was there with seven brethren of his own Order. Cardinal Ugolino, who was at the papal court at Perugia, was also present. The cardinal was very impressed when he saw the multitude of the brethren. "These are the legions of Christ," he said. The brethren held their chapter in the open air, and little huts, made of matted straw, had been put up to accommodate them. This chapter came to be known as "the Chapter of the Mats".

When all were gathered together Francis, filled with the Holy Spirit, spoke to them. "We have promised great things to God," he said, "but God has promised still greater things to us. Let us be true to our promises, and we know that he will be true to his. The pleasures of this world are short-lived, and perpetual pain is their reward; but the pains of this world are also short-lived, and their reward is everlasting joy."[39]

He then went on to urge them to be true servants of Lady Poverty, and to have unbounded trust in God's goodness. "I am commanding you," he continued, "in virtue of holy obedience, to have no cares about earthly things, or about what you will eat or drink, but only to think about prayer and the praises of God: cast all your cares upon him, who has so much care for you." St Dominic admitted his surprise at this holy improvidence, until he noticed how the local people began to come from the towns and villages, bearing food and drink for the brethren, and regarding it a privilege to be able to serve these holy men. He turned to St Francis, and went on his knees before him. "Indeed," he said, "God looks after the brethren in their holy poverty. I did not understand. From now on I promise it: I also will observe the same evangelical poverty."[40]

Notes on the four plates that follow

97 A FRANCISCAN OF LA VERNA PREPARES FOR THE QUEST
The "quest" is the Franciscan word for a journey undertaken with the object of begging
for the community.

98 CONVENTUALS IN THE CLOISTER GARTH AT SAN FRANCESCO
AT ASSISI

99 BROTHER LEONARD WITH HIS TURTLE-DOVES AT FONTE
COLOMBO

100 CAPUCHINS IN CHOIR AT CELLE DI CORTONA
To love God, to love poverty, to love all creatures: this is the legacy of Francis, still treasured
by his sons.

98

"To enlighten them that sit in darkness, and in the shadow of death." Francis could not forget the people in strange and distant lands who had never heard the Gospel, and once more he determined to go and preach to them. He commissioned Brother Matthew of Narni, a man of great piety, to receive in his name novices at the Porziuncola; and he instructed Brother Gregory of Naples, a very learned man, to go round all the provinces and encourage the brethren. He himself then took thirteen companions and they sailed on a crusaders' ship from Ancona to Cyprus and Acre, and so to Egypt. Here they met the crusading army. Francis was greatly distressed to see their immoral behaviour, and he also witnessed a terrible defeat of the Christian forces. He asked the cardinal-legate who was there for permission to go and preach the Word of God to the sultan, and he hoped thereby to die a martyr's death. He eventually gained admittance to the presence of Melek el Kamil, the head of Islam, crying "Soldan! Soldan!" Contrary to all expectation, the sultan received him and his companions in a most friendly manner, and heard him willingly. But the sultan was not converted; so Francis returned to Acre, where a number of clerics joined the Order. From Acre he made a pilgrimage to the Holy Land, and visited the holy places with great devotion. But then he hastened back to Italy, for he had heard reports that his Order was in danger through dissensions among the brethren and misinterpretations of his Rule. He landed at Burano near Venice, tired and ill. This was the beginning of a time of severe trial for him.

Notes on the four plates that follow

101 BURANO NEAR VENICE
In the time of Francis this island, together with the neighbouring island of Torcello, formed an important harbour. The harbour has long been silted up, and the islands now have a placid existence on the lagoon. It was at Burano that Francis came ashore on his return from the East.

102 SAN FRANCESCO DEL DESERTO
By this lagoon St Francis spent several weeks on his return.

103 THE WATER ENTRANCE TO THE FRIARY ON THE ISLAND

104 SAINT FRANCIS' ISLE
The sea-breeze still sings in the cypresses, as it did when he was here.

THE THREAT TO LADY POVERTY

While Francis was away in the East, some of the brethren at home asked Pope Honorius III to issue commendatory letters, which would ensure for them the favour and protection of the bishops of the world. The Pope duly issued the letters. But this was not at all what Francis wanted: he wanted the brethren to win the favour of the bishops and the Christian world by the humility and piety of their lives, and not by any official letters of the Pope. Another scheme that was proposed while the Saint was away was that the Friars Minor should get the same legal privileges that the older Orders enjoyed and, moreover, that any member of the Order who did not agree to this proposal should be dismissed. Small wonder, then, that many of the brethren were filled with joy when the Saint returned.

On his way from Burano to Assisi Francis visited Bologna, where he was distressed to find a great change of heart in many of the brethren. The Provincial of Lombardy, Peter Stacia, who had won his doctorate at the University of Bologna, had just completed a large house of studies in that city, and he apparently regarded this building as the property of the Order. For Francis this was an open betrayal of Lady Poverty, and he refused to set foot over the threshold. He ordered all the brethren to leave the house at once, and would not even consider leaving the sick behind.

As he drew near to the Porziuncola he was overcome by weakness, and had to mount a donkey. His companion was Brother Leonard, formerly a nobleman of Assisi, who grumbled to himself that he had to go on foot. Suddenly Francis leaped off the donkey. "Take my place, Brother," he said, "it isn't right that a nobleman like you should walk, while I ride." The Brother saw that the Saint had read his thoughts. He felt covered with shame, and throwing himself at the Saint's feet, admitted his fault.

Notes on the four plates that follow

105 THE ROMAN AMPHITHEATRE AT VERONA
On the way from Venice to Assisi St Francis also passed through Verona, a city with many ancient monuments which were there in Francis' time as they are today.

106 SAN ZENO AT VERONA
The bronze doors of the Benedictine abbey church.

107 BASALT CRUCIFIX AT BOLOGNA
Crosses were erected on four ancient pillars in front of the gateways of the city. This one was at the Porta Ravennata, and is now in San Petronio at Bologna.

108 A CYPRESS IN THE CLOISTER GARTH OF THE FRANCISCAN FRIARY AT VILLA VERUCCHIO
It is believed that Francis planted this tree on his homeward journey.

[54]

105

It was not that all innovations were bad for the Order. A decree of Pope Honorius III about the same time ordained that in future no brother was to be admitted to vows without a year of probation, nor pass to another Order, nor travel about without written permission of his superior. This meant that the work of St Francis was saved from many abuses which had either arisen or threatened to do so.

As the Order developed, the question of studies became more and more urgent. Francis was a man of quick and penetrating intelligence, but not by nature a scholar, and he had given much thought to the matter of studies. For him, the only value of study was to increase the knowledge and love of God. And because he felt that the pursuit of study often made the student proud and self-opinionated, at the beginning he refused to allow the brethren to possess books at all.

At the general chapter of 1221 there was present a Portuguese brother, whose manner was so quiet and retiring that he seemed in no way marked out for a career. The Provincial of Lombardy, Brother Gratian, took pity on him and accepted him for his province, sending him to the little friary of San Paolo, on a hilltop near Forlí. Here he occupied himself with contemplation and humble tasks about the house. On the occasion of an ordination the brethren of San Paolo, including the Portuguese Brother Anthony, were invited to a supper together with a few Dominicans. No one present was prepared to make a speech, and Brother Anthony was therefore called upon to do so. To the astonishment of all he showed himself to be most learned in theology and a brilliant speaker. Now, instead of working in the kitchen, he began to occupy the principal pulpits of the land, and soon came to be known as the "hammer of the heretics". Francis found in Anthony a theologian after his own heart, and he wrote him a letter: "To Brother Anthony, my master. I am delighted that you are teaching theology to the brethren, and in particular that you are doing it so that (according to our Rule) their studies in no way obscure their spirit of prayer."[41] Anthony died young, worn out by his labours for the Kingdom of God, but the fame of his sanctity lived on, growing through the centuries. And now the shrine of St Anthony of Padua, the learned man whose help is sought for the most humble needs, is visited by pilgrims from all over the world. The wonder-worker's tomb is at Padua, but his devotees are to be found in every quarter of the earth.

Notes on the four plates that follow

Above: the authorization for the establishment of the novitiate, September 22nd 1220, issued at Orvieto.

Below: the document granting permission to the brethren to celebrate Mass everywhere, even during the time of an interdict.

110

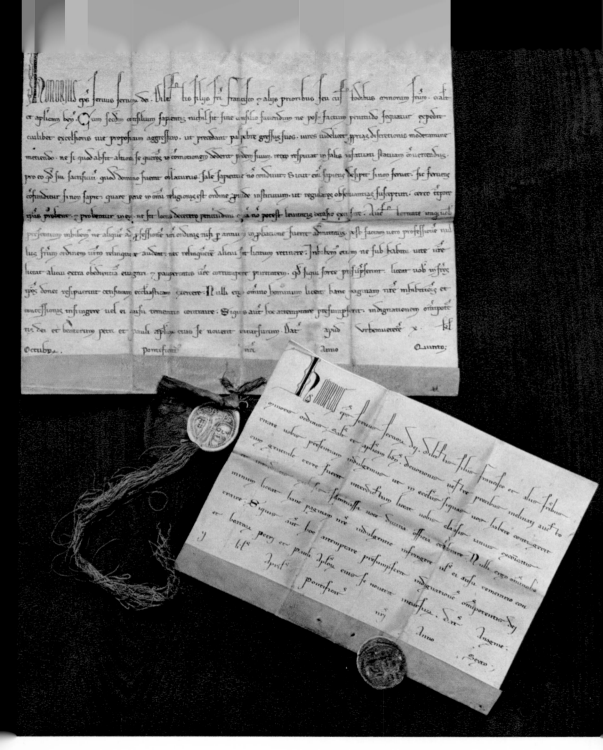

THE THIRD ORDER

Among the sons and daughters of St Francis there were many who did not leave hearth and home, but led their lives following him in spirit. Property was for them a loan from God, and a means by which they could do good in the world and help the poor. They set out to live a life of peace with all men, of justice towards their superiors and inferiors, and of abstemiousness with regard to the things of this world. Francis allowed them to keep as much property as was necessary to their station. In these ways they were to keep their minds on eternal things, and to avoid quarrels and dissensions.

One of the first to adopt this mode of life in the world was Count Orlando, who, after making the gift of La Verna, felt himself greatly attached to the brethren. Another person who placed herself under Francis' direction was the rich widow of ancient lineage, Jacoba of Settesoli, whom Francis used to call "Brother Jacoba". It was presumably to groups of people such as these that St Francis originally wrote the document known as "The Letter to all Christians". This is a rule governing the interior life: it enjoins the observance not only of the Commandments, but also of the Counsels, it urges obedience and insists on justice and restitution, it recommends penance and it ends with a call to praise of the Holy Trinity, God the highest and almighty, who alone is truly wonderful and good. The oldest form of the Rule of the Franciscan Third Order dates from 1221, and regulates the interior and exterior life of the Brethren and Sisters of Penance. The first group of Tertiaries in Florence set up a hospital in the city, where the brethren and sisters themselves tended the poor.[42]

One day at Todi, Francis met a woman going down to the Tiber, carrying a basket. He asked her what she was doing, and she replied that she was taking some washing down to the river. "No," he said, "you are going down to the river to drown the result of your sin. Give me the child: I will look after it." And he took the child. He then found in Todi a good woman who undertook to nurse it; and this was the beginning of the orphanage conducted by the Third Order in that town.

At Poggibonsi Francis found a friend in the rich merchant Luchesio, with his wife, who because of her kindness was known to the people as Buona Donna. These two sold most of their property and gave the proceeds to the poor, and then sought from the hands of St Francis the habit of penance. Thenceforth Luchesio himself looked after the small property they had kept, and he threw open his house to the poor, always serving them at table with his own hands before sitting down himself. He would seek out the sick and carry them on his own shoulders to his house, where Buona Donna nursed them. If they had given up everything, instead of being able to help the beggars they would have become beggars themselves. It happened that the two of them fell ill together and were near to death. Buona Donna prayed that her husband would be able to stand by her as she died, whereupon he received new strength and was able to console her at the point of death. As soon as she had passed into eternal life, her husband laid down and followed her. Thus the two of them who had done God's work on earth together, even in death were not divided.

Notes on the four plates that follow

113 A CONTEMPORARY CRUCIFIX IN THE CATHEDRAL AT TODI
It is not unlike the Crucifix at San Damiano, which spoke to St Francis.

114 CANNARA
Where Francis wrote the Rule of the Third Order.

115 A TERTIARY PROCESSION
This typical procession is at Rivotorto, and the Tertiary banner is being carried.

116 POGGIBONSI
Where Luchesio and Buona Donna lived in the spirit of poverty and charity, and so laid the foundations of one of the early groups of Tertiaries.

116

The confusion that arose in the Order while the founder was away in the East moved him on his return to go and see the Pope. "I will go and place the Order of Friars Minor in the hands of the Holy Roman Church," he said, "if the Church has charge of the Order, no harm can come to it. And indeed, our Mother the Church will herself profit from our poverty, and the spirit of the Gospel will breathe forth afresh within her."[43]

Francis waited humbly at the entrance to the palace, until the Pope came out. Francis bowed before him and said: "Holy Father, may God give you peace!" The Pope answered: "God bless you, my son." Then Francis said: "My Lord, because of your high office and your many duties, little people cannot come and ask to speak to you as often as they should. Will you give me one of my lords the cardinals who could listen to my troubles and those of my Order and advise me as your representative?" "Which one shall I give you, my son?" said the Pope. "Give me His Eminence the Cardinal of Ostia," said St Francis. The Pope agreed, and after this, Cardinal Ugolino took the Order more than ever under his protection.[44]

Francis asked the cardinal for permission to retire from the government of the Order, so as to give himself time to compose a new Rule. Peter of Cattaneo was appointed Vicar of the Order at the Porziuncola, there to assume government in the place of Francis. At the same time messages were sent out to all the provinces, summoning the brethren to a general chapter at Pentecost of the next year, 1221. But before the assembly of the chapter Peter of Cattaneo was dead, and was buried at the Porziuncola.

In his place the Provincial of Syria was chosen, Brother Elias. Brother Elias had in his heart a very great and genuine admiration for the founder, and both Francis and Cardinal Ugolino had great hopes that his determination and shrewd judgement would bring back peace to the Order. But it soon became evident that his main purpose was to place the Order well to the fore in the public eye. After he had cared for the Saint during his last days with the utmost devotion, he had a huge church and friary built over his tomb, as a permanent memorial, and it must be said that in spite of its massive proportions it does somehow convey the spirit of the Poverello. Unfortunately, Brother Elias became involved in the political conflict between the Pope and the emperor, and, having taken the side of the Emperor Frederick II, was excommunicated. In 1239 he was removed from the office of Minister-General, and he retired to Cortona, where in his early days he had founded the little friary known as Celle di Cortona, and later had built a huge church in honour of St Francis. It was in this church that he was buried on April 22nd 1253.[45]

Notes on the four plates that follow

117 INSCRIPTION ON THE TOMB OF PETER OF CATTANEO, THE
FIRST VICAR OF THE ORDER
The inscription is in the wall of the Porziuncola. The text reads: *Anno Domini MCCXXI, VI Id.Martii, Corpus Fratris P. Catanii, qui hic requiescit, migravit ad Dominum, animam cujus benedicat Dominus, Amen.* "In the year of Our Lord 1221, on March 10th, the body of Brother P. Catanii, who rests here, went to the Lord, and may the Lord bless his soul, Amen."

118 A RELIC OF THE TRUE CROSS AT CORTONA
This was a personal present to Brother Elias from the Eastern Emperor John Ducas, who gave it to him at Constantinople in 1239.

119 THE REVERSE OF THE RELIC IN ITS BAROQUE FRAME

120 CORTONA
Where Brother Elias finally settled. His tomb is behind the high altar of the church which he built in honour of St Francis.

[60]

120

FRANCIS FINALLY WRITES THE RULE

Since there were many brethren who were not satisfied with the Second Rule of 1221, and representations were made from many quarters, Francis finally decided to write the Rule afresh. Chief among those who were calling for a revision were the learned adherents of the movement to which Brother Elias belonged. They hoped in particular for mitigations in the matter of poverty. On the one hand they desired that the Order as a whole should be allowed to possess property, but on the other hand they felt that a greater strictness was required in monastic observances and in matters such as fasting. Yet Francis was unwilling to limit the freedom of the Gospel by any such particular legislation.

Francis left the Porziuncola with Brother Leo and Brother Bonizzo, and at Monte Rainerio, amid much prayer and fasting, wrote the new Rule. After a short time he went back to the Porziuncola and handed what he had written to Brother Elias of Cortona. Within a few days Brother Elias declared that the document had been lost. Francis, undaunted in his pursuit of the original ideal of the Order, returned once more to Monte Rainerio, and this time dictated the new Rule to Brother Leo. Meanwhile, brethren of the new movement followed him to his retreat and insisted that their requirements should find a place in the new Rule. Francis, however, would not give way, stating that God had called him and the Order to the path of the strictest poverty, a path which he could in no way abandon. The others then told him that they would not recognize the new Rule if it failed to include their proposals.[46]

Notes on the four plates that follow

121 CHAPEL OF ST MARY MAGDALENE AT FONTE COLOMBO
Fonte Colombo was previously known as Monte Rainerio. This chapel goes back to the time of the Saint.

122 ST FRANCIS' GROTTO
It was here that he wrote the Third Rule.

123 OAKS NEAR THE GROTTO

124 THE CHAPEL OF THE MIRACULOUS SPRING
The chapel marks the spot of the miraculous spring, which gave the name Fonte Colombo to Monte Rainerio. It lies on the thickly wooded hillside on the way up to the friary.

121

124

PAPAL APPROVAL OF THE RULE

Francis wanted this Third Rule to be fully approved by the Church. He therefore set off on foot for Rome. As he crossed the threshold of St Peter's he must surely have remembered how it was here that he first understood what real poverty meant. Probably he received hospitality from "Brother Jacoba". A small building near the palace of Septimius Severus is still shown, claiming to be where Francis lodged. Francis first took his Rule to his friend Cardinal Ugolino. The cardinal probably suggested a few alterations, and the Roman curia then apparently introduced some mitigations and a few general prescriptions, and put the whole thing into proper legal language. Although, therefore, the document no longer immediately reflects the warmth of Francis' own words, it may be said that not one of his main ideas has been lost. The brethren are still obliged to keep absolute poverty; whoever enters the Order must first give his property to the poor; the brethren must be content with the poorest clothing, they must be peace-loving and humble, and not pass judgement on others; their work must never obscure the spirit of prayer; they must beg humbly for alms; none may own houses or lands, but must be as strangers and pilgrims in the world.[47]

Pope Honorius III gave his formal written approval to the Rule on November 29th 1223.

Notes on the four plates that follow

125 MEDIEVAL BUILDING IN ROME
It is believed that Francis lodged in this little tower. In the background are the ruins of the palace of Septimius Severus.

126 THE CLOISTERS AT THE LATERAN
The Lateran Palace was at the time the papal residence.

127 THE ORIGINAL OF THE PAPAL BULL CONFIRMING THE RULE
Now preserved in the treasury at San Francesco at Assisi.

128 SAN SALVATORE NEAR SPOLETO
Between Assisi and Rome St Francis may well have visited this early Christian sanctuary, built in the 5th century on the ruins of a pagan temple. Such a building is symbolic of the edifice raised by Francis on the ruins of a corrupted world.

[64]

HONORIVS eps seruus seruorum dei. Dilectis filiis fri
et honestis [f]r petentium desiderijs fauorem beniuolum impertin. Eapropter
notatam presentibus auctoritate uobis .fica confirmamus et presentis
et [con]silicet du nri ihuxpi sctm euuangelium obseruare uiuendo inobedientia sine
ecclie Roman et alijs fres teneantur fri francisco et eius successoribus obedire De
uouerint eos ad suos ministros prouinciales quibus solummodo et non ali
bet omia credant et uelint ea fidelit conficere et usq in finem firmit obser
epi uoto contingit iam emisso et illud sic etatis uxores quod non possit
facere non potuerint sufficit eis bona uoluntas. Et caueant fres et eorum mi
requiratur. Licentiam habeant ministri mittendi eos ad aliquos deum timentes
cingulum et uacas et capione usq ad cingulum nisi eisdem ministris aliud
de ista religione seire iuxta mandatum dni quia secundum sctm euuangelium nemo mittens
qui diuerni tibe Et qui necessitate coguntur possunt portare calciamenta. Et fres
iudicent hoies quos uident mollib uestimentis colloratis indutos uti cibis et potib
officia secundum ordinem sce Romane ecclie excepto psalterio eiqui habere poterit breuiaria. Laici uo
pro completorio sctem et orent pro defunctis. et ieiunent a festo omnium scorum usq ad
carie eam ieiunant benedicti sint a dno. et qui idlum norsint astricti, sed aliam usq
ieiunio corporali. Insulo uo moneo et exhortor fres meos in dno ihuxpo ut quando uada
res omnibus fiant decat Et non debeant equitare nisi manifesta necessitate ut infirmi
fres no recipiant pecuniam. Precipio firmit frib uniuersis ut nullomodo denarios ut pecu
tollecetur curantg eis et secundum loca et tempora et frigidas regiones sicut necessitati uiderint
et deuote. ita qd exclusi otio animae inimico sce oronis et deuotionis spin no extinguant cui debe
uos fori et puptatis saissime sectatores. Quod nichil approprient sibi fres. et de helemosina
buitate dno famulantes uadant pro helemosina confident nec oportet eos uerecundari quia dn
sctri. uirtutib sublimauit hec sit portio uia que ducat in terra uiuentium. cui dilectissimi
pacem interse. Et secure manifestit unus alteri necessitatem suam. Quia si mat nutra et
sicut uellent sibi fuum Oe penitentia fribus peccantibus imponenda. Siqui frum insug
fres ad eos reuertere quomcatus poterint sine mora. Ipsi uo ministri si pbri sint cui miser
et cauere debent ne irascantur et conturbentur propter peccatum alicuius. quia ira et
anium de fribus istius religionis teneantur semper habere generalem ministrum et

WITH THE BRETHREN AT RIETI

Once more Francis returned to the hill-country of Rieti, where the steep mountain-sides and the deep caverns were the only witnesses of his penance and his prayer. He loved especially a piece of wild country above Poggio Bustone: the place where shortly after his conversion he had wept over his sins under a huge overhanging cliff. When he had been scarcely able to bear the recollection of the follies of his youth, he suddenly broke into a joyful song of praise, and he then knew without a doubt that all the sins of his youth had been forgiven. As he made his way, through the bare and forbidding valleys, back to the dwellings of men, he heard again and again ringing through the clear air the message: "Your prayer has been heard: your sins are forgiven!" Still today we can read these words above the stairway leading to his cell at Poggio Bustone.

John of Velitta, a tertiary who well knew the Saint's love of solitude and had always hoped to offer him hospitality, made him a gift of some caves high up on a mountain near Greccio, and also built a cell for the brethren in a wood nearby.[48]

Francis was once going to keep Easter with the brethren there, and he found the table richly laid with tablecloths, crockery and suchlike, which the brethren had borrowed for the feast-day from a rich friend. Francis waited until the brethren had begun their meal, and then he went in with an old hat and a beggar's staff, and said: "For the love of Christ, give an alms to a poor pilgrim!" The brethren invited him to sit down with them at table, but Francis seized a dish and sat down on the ground. "This is how a real Friar Minor should do it," he said. "When I saw your table so well-appointed, I thought this could not be the table of men who beg their alms from door to door. We, more than any other Order, should love the poverty of Our Lord." The brethren took the Saint's words very much to heart, and several of them began to sob, saying they felt that they had seen Our Lord.[49]

Notes on the four plates that follow

129 VIEW TOWARDS POGGIO BUSTONE AT THE FOOT OF THE
     SABINE MOUNTAINS
     Seen from the Vale of Rieti.

130 THE FRIARY ON THE SLOPES OF GRECCIO
     The friary looks out over the Vale of Rieti.

131 THE CHRISTMAS GROTTO AT GRECCIO
     (See next chapter)

132 THE VALLEY TO THE EAST OF POGGIO BUSTONE
     The steep, bare valley goes sharply down towards the plain.

[66]

FRANCIS THE DEACON

Three years before his death, as Francis was spending Christmas at Greccio, he said to Brother John Velitta: "This Christmas I would like really to bring home to the people of Greccio what the birth of Christ at Bethlehem was like. They ought to see how poor he was, lying there on straw, with the ox and the ass beside him." All the brethren in the district were accordingly invited, and the local people prepared candles and torches for Christmas night.

The crib was put up and the ox and ass were there. The woods and whole hillside echoed the songs of the people. At the solemn Mass Francis was the deacon, and robed in the rich vestments of the liturgy he sang the Christmas Gospel with great joy. He then spoke to the people of the birth of Christ, and how this was the happiest event that had ever occurred and the source of divine grace to mankind. It was said that as he pronounced the word "Bethlehem" his voice sounded like the bleating of a lamb, and that every time he uttered the Name of Jesus he appeared overwhelmed with love, and seemed to savour the sweet sound upon his lips.[50]

One man said that when he first saw the crib the image of the Child looked like a dead child, but that as soon as Francis had come in, the Child seemed to come to life. It was as if the Child Jesus lay neglected and forgotten in the hearts of so many men, only to come to life anew within them when they are touched by God's grace and the labours of his servant.[51]

Notes on the four plates that follow

133   A SANDAL OF ST FRANCIS
       He wore sandals of soft natural leather when he officiated as deacon at the altar. The relic is
       preserved at Santa Chiara at Assisi.

134   A PIECE OF THE HABIT OF ST FRANCIS
       St Francis chose cloth of rough coarse wool, black and white, for his usual garment. (Sacristy
       of San Francesco, Assisi.

135   DEACON'S ALB, WORN BY ST FRANCIS
       For liturgical attire, he had fine, white and richly embroidered linen. (Santa Chiara, Assisi.)

136   CHALICE AND PATEN
       Used by St Francis as deacon, at the ablutions at Mass.

[68]

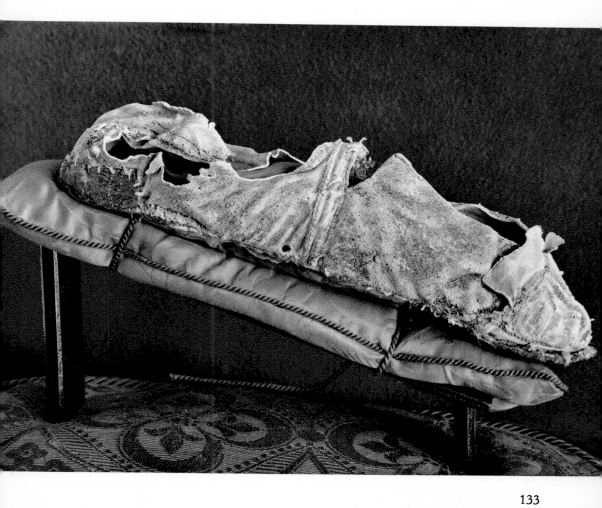

133

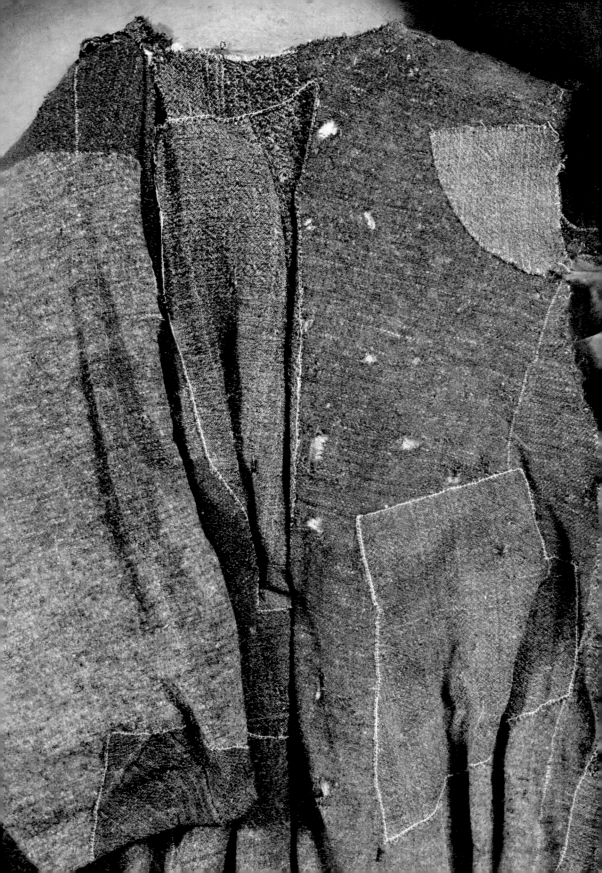

136

THE STIGMATA

Francis had not forgotten the gift of Count Orlando. On the feast of the Assumption in 1224, Francis, together with a few of the brethren with whom he was very intimate, made for La Verna. Across the plains they went, past the villages, through the woods and up to the wild rock-lands. Francis chose a place alone, apart from the others, in a rough shack under a beech-tree. No one was to come to him except Brother Leo, who brought him bread and water and ministered to him as a priest. Brother Leo often found him in ecstasy, raised above the ground. He would then kiss the holy man's feet, and say: "O God, have mercy on me a sinner, and let me receive grace through the merits of this holy man!" One day Francis withdrew to a still more lonely spot, where he found a ledge of rock with a hundred-foot drop below it, and a deep chasm separating it from the mountain. Across this chasm they threw a tree-trunk to form a bridge, but even Brother Leo was not allowed to go across except when Francis gave him express permission. Temptations and ecstasies succeeded one another, and once it seemed to Francis as if a dazzling angel came and played music to him and he lost consciousness altogether.

On the feast of the Exaltation of the Cross he had a vision which filled him with fear: it was a vision of at once a man and a seraph: the arms were extended, the feet placed one upon the other, the body was fastened to a cross. Two wings appeared above the head, two wings were spread in flight, two wings covered the body. Suddenly Francis felt his body pierced with unspeakable pain, and gradually the vision faded. When Francis came to himself, he found the wounds in his hands and feet, and as it were nails in the wounds. The heads of the nails, black, were in the palms of his hands and on the upper part of his feet, while the points, bent round, appeared on the backs of his hands and the soles of his feet. And there was a wound in his right side. He felt compelled to tell the brethren what had happened, but he showed the wounds only to Brother Leo.[52] He also asked Brother Leo to bless the stone on which the seraph had

[69]

stood, and then to anoint it, first with water, then with wine, then with oil, and finally with balsam.[53] The place is still kept as a holy place by the brethren.

Notes on the four plates that follow

137 VIEW FROM THE CLIFFS OF LA VERNA
     The view extends over the plateau of the same name

138 IN THE BEECH FOREST OF LA VERNA

139 A ROCK LEDGE NEAR THE PLACE OF THE STIGMATA
     It was probably on a cliff not unlike this one that Francis was praying when the seraphic vision appeared.

140 A PIECE OF CHAMOIS LEATHER
     Francis later used this piece of leather to cover the bleeding wound in his side.

140

FAREWELL TO LA VERNA

Brother Masseo has left us a moving account of the Saint's departure from La Verna. The original manuscript is a treasured possession of the friary at La Verna.

"Our dearest Father had decided to bid farewell to the holy mountain on September 30th 1224, the feast of St Jerome. My lord Orlando, the Count of Chiusi, had sent up a beast for him to ride on, since on account of the wounds in his feet he could not walk. Early that morning he heard Mass as usual in the little chapel of Our Lady of the Angels. Then he summoned the brethren and commanded them under obedience: they were to remain lovingly together, to give themselves to prayer, and to recite their Office by day and by night. Then he commended to their care the holy mountain: never were the brethren, now or in the future, to use this mountain for any secular purposes: on the contrary, they were always to look upon it as a holy place, and he would bless quite specially those who lived here or looked after the holy place reverently. To me he then said: 'Brother Masseo, I want you to know that it is my desire that only good religious should live here—the best of my Order. Oh, Brother Masseo, what more can I say?'

"Then he began to take his leave: 'Farewell, Brother Masseo,' he said, 'Farewell. Farewell, farewell, Brother Angelo.' And he said the same to Brother Silvester and Brother Illuminato. Then he said: 'Live in peace, my dearest sons, and God bless you. I am going away, but my heart stays with you. I am going with Brother Leo, the lamb of God. I am going to Santa Maria degli Angeli, and I shall never come back. Now I must go, farewell, and love one another! Farewell, holy mountain. Farewell, Mountain of La Verna. Farewell, dear Brother falcon, and thank you for your kindness to me. Farewell, mighty rock of Sasso spicco. I shall never see you again. Farewell, little chapel of Our Lady: to you, o Mother of the Word, I commend these sons of mine.' And so he left, weeping, and he took our hearts with him. I, Brother Masseo, have written this through my tears. God bless us all."[54]

Notes on the eight plates that follow

141 ▷

148

TWO LETTERS OF ST FRANCIS

The handwriting is that of a man whose great strength lay in his love. We feel the effort at the beginning of almost every word. A delicate man, tired out; yet with a heart that never tired. Determination, generosity, a kind of shining trust: these things we can see in the handwriting. The Saint is not known to have written many letters, but two are addressed to Brother Leo, "the lamb of God". One is the famous blessing left to his friend, carefully preserved at San Francesco at Assisi; and the other, addressed to this beloved disciple, is since 1902 treasured in the cathedral archives at Spoleto.

Of actual autographs of the Saint only these two have remained, but in them we have both in the handwriting itself and in the content of the writings almost living witnesses to his character.

The blessing for Brother Leo: "God bless you, and keep you! May he look on you and give you mercy; may he turn to you and give you peace. God bless you, Brother Leo!"

On the reverse of the sheet is written in the same hand: "Thou alone art the holy Lord and God, doer of wonders. Thou art strong, thou art great, thou art high above all. Thou art almighty, holy Father, King of heaven and earth. Thou art Three and thou art One, the King of kings. Thou art good, thou art all goodness, the highest good, Lord, one true God. Thou art love, thou art wisdom, thou art humility, patience and beauty; thou art safety, peace and joy. Thou art our hope, thou art justice and equity, thou our riches and sufficiency. Thou art our refuge and our strength, thou the unfathomable, great and adorable goodness!"[55]

The other letter: "Brother Leo, your brother Francis sends you peace and greeting. I am telling you, as a mother tells her son, that all the things we talked about on the journey I can put into a few words of advice, so that you don't have to come to me for advice about everything; because my advice to you is that in whatever way you are pleasing the Lord God, and following his footsteps and his poverty, you are doing it with the blessing of the Lord God and in obedience to me. But if your spirit has any need of further consolation and you want to come to me, then, Leo, just come."[56]

Amid the tenderness of this letter there is the firm determination that holy poverty shall stand, come what may.

Notes on the four plates that follow

149 THE AUTOGRAPH OF ST FRANCIS' BLESSING TO BROTHER LEO
Preserved at San Francesco at Assisi.

150 THE OBVERSE OF THE PARCHMENT

151 THE REVERSE OF THE PARCHMENT

152 THE SAINT'S LETTER TO BROTHER LEO
Preserved since 1902 in the cathedral archives at Spoleto.
Transcription (added by the translator) from the photograph, with abbreviations spelt out and punctuation inserted

> f.leo f.francissco tuo sa-
> lutem & pacem. ita dico tibi,
> fili mei, sicut mater, quia
> omnia verba que diximus
> in via, breviter in hoc verba
> dispono & consilio, & non
> . . . . . oportet propter
> consilium venire ad me;
> quia ita consilio tibi, in qo-
> cunque modo melius . . .
> . . . . placere domino
> deo & sequi vestigia & pa-
> upertatem suam, faciatis
> cum beneditione domini
> dei & mea obedientia;
> & si tibi est necesarium
> animam tuam propter aliam
> consolationem tuam & v . ..
> . . . . ad me .
> . . . .

[74]

149

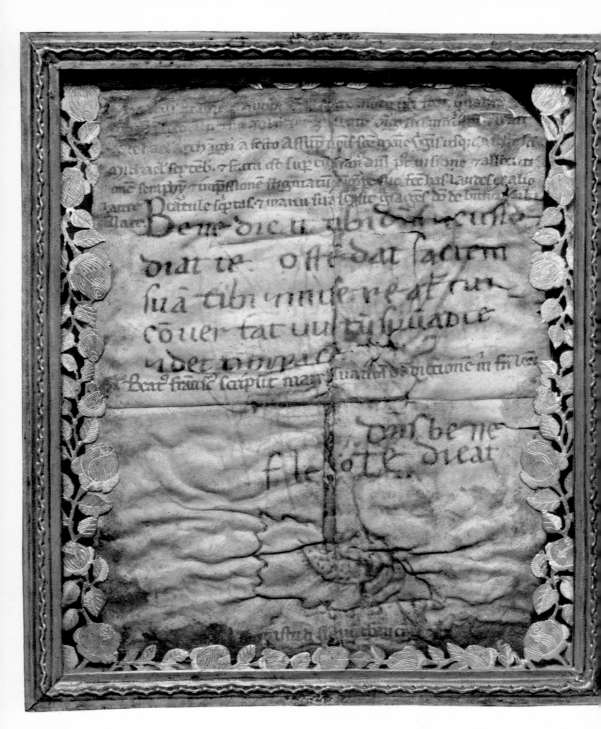

150

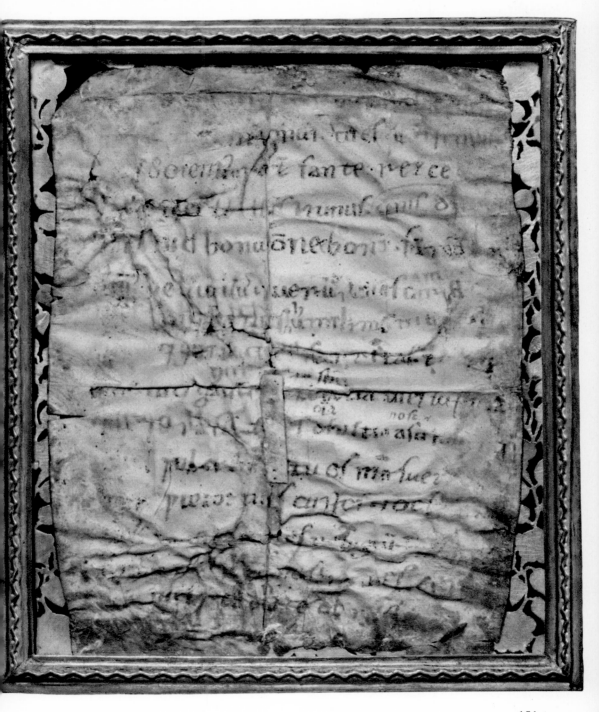

ff leo f fra cis sco tuo sa
lute y pace. Ita dico tibi.
fili me i sicut mat. qa
oia vba que diximus
uia. breuit inbc vba
eis po nouco si lio yn
apor at pt
co filiu ue mne ame.
q ma co filio tibi iqo
cuq modo me li u sa
de t placerne dio
eo i seque ffi gã
pta te sua faci a ti
cu be ne di tio ne dni
y me a obe die nca
tu bi e it ne ce i a
m. ma tu ã pt dlu ã
o lu tio ne tua y

THE CANTICLE OF THE SUN

Brother Francis was in the nuns' garden at San Damiano. He was weighed down with illness and with many sorrows. Suddenly he broke into a song of praise, a song of all creatures praising their Creator, a song for all men to hear with joy.*

Most high omnipotent good Lord,
    Thine are praise, glory and honour and all benediction,
To thee, alone, Most High, do they belong:
    And no man is there, worthy thee to name.

Praise be to thee, my Lord, with all thy creatures,
    Chiefest of all, Sir Brother Sun,
Who is our day, through whom thou givest light:
    Beautiful is he; radiant, with great splendour:
Of thee, Most High, he is a true revealer.

Praise be to thee, my Lord, for Sister Moon and for the stars;
In heaven hast thou formed them, bright, precious and fair.

Praise be to thee, my Lord, for Brother Wind, and for the air
    and for the cloud, for clear sky and all weathers,
By which thou givest nourishment to all thy creatures.

* The translation is that given in Fr Cuthbert's *Life*, admirably rendering the original Italian.

Praise be to thee, my Lord, for Sister Water; she
Most useful is, and humble, precious and pure.

Praise be to thee, my Lord, for Brother Fire; by whom
Thou lightest up the night:
And fair is he and merry, mighty and strong.

Praise be to thee, my Lord, for our Sister, Mother Earth,
The which sustains and keeps us:
She brings forth divers fruits,
The many-hued flowers and grass.

About this time a heated dissension broke out between the citizens of Assisi and the bishop. Francis summoned the opposing parties, and had the Canticle of the Sun sung to them by the brethren. At the end he added a new verse about peace, and all present were so moved that they asked pardon of one another and gave each other the kiss of peace.

The new verse was as follows:

> Praise be to thee, my Lord, for those who pardon grant for
>   love of thee,
>   And weakness bear and buffetings:
> Blessed are they who in peace abide,
>   For by thee, Most High, they shall be crowned.

When Francis felt that his end was not far away, once more he asked that the brethren should sing to him the Canticle of the Sun. And when they came to the end, Francis added yet another verse, this time in praise of Sister Death:

> Praise be to thee, my Lord, for our Sister, Bodily Death, from
>   whom no living man can flee;
>   Woe is to them who die in mortal sin.
> But blessed they who shall find themselves in thy most holy will:
>   To them the second death shall do no ill.

And the concluding verse that was sung each time was this:

> O creatures all, praise and bless my Lord and grateful be,
>   And serve him with deep humility.[57]

Notes on the four plates that follow

153 CENTRAL SECTION OF THE ALTAR-PIECE AT CITTÀ DI
CASTELLO
Francis had probably knelt before this majestic figure shortly before he sang "Most high
omnipotent good Lord".

154 SUNSET OVER THE TRASIMENE LAKE
In the distance is the Isola Maggiore, where Francis once kept a forty days' fast.
"Praise be to thee, my Lord, with all thy creatures,
    Chiefest of all, Sir Brother Sun!"

155 FLAME IN THE FIREPLACE AT FONTE COLOMBO
"Praise be to thee, my Lord, for Brother Fire!"

156 THE SEA NEAR CIVITAVECCHIA
"Praise be to thee, my Lord, for Brother Wind, and for the air and for the cloud, for clear
sky and all weathers!"

154

Francis left San Damiano, where St Clare had looked after him with sisterly care, and where the Canticle of the Sun had been begotten. Now he returned once more to his beloved Vale of Rieti. On the way he was again taken seriously ill, and he was glad to accept the hospitality offered to him by the priest at the church of San Fabiano at La Foresta. The priest was very poor and only managed to keep alive by the produce of his vineyard, which in good years would yield twelve measures of wine. But as soon as the news spread that Francis was there, crowds of people began to come, as if on pilgrimage, to see him at La Foresta. The pilgrims came from far and near, and many of them satisfied their hunger by eating the grapes from the priest's vineyard. The poor priest was very upset, because he saw his only source of revenue being devoured; but Francis consoled him, promising to make good any loss if the vineyard did not yield this year a good twenty measures. Soon it was autumn and the priest was gathering in his harvest. He was greatly astonished when he came to store the wine and found the yield to be a full twenty measures.

The Saint's entry into the gallant city of Rieti was a triumphal progress. The news of the stigmata, which God had impressed upon the body of his servant, had gone before him, and everyone wanted to pay honour to the man whom God had so honoured. The bishop had received Francis in his palace, and many people brought their sick to the palace, to be healed. A number of cures took place. Then Francis asked to be taken to Monte Rainerio (now Fonte Colombo) to find more peace and solitude. He was suffering much from his eyes at the time, and for his relief the local doctor proposed a cauterization of the temples. As they were heating the iron in the fire, Francis said: "O Brother Fire, among all creatures God has made you noble and useful to mankind. Be now gentle with me, for I have always loved you, and always will, for the love of him who made you." He then made a sign of the Cross over the red-hot iron and allowed the operation to be carried out without a murmur. The brethren in their anxiety had left the room, but now they came back, and Francis greeted them: "O you faint-hearted men of little faith," he said, "why did you run away? I felt no pain or burning, and if it was not enough, let them start again." But the operation brought little relief. Later they tried opening the vein above the ear, and finally they tried piercing both ears with a red-hot iron. But it was of little avail: his bodily strength was failing; yet the weaker he became, the stronger his spirit seemed to grow, joyfully awaiting the end.

Notes on the four plates that follow

157 ST CLARE'S GARDEN AT SAN DAMIANO
Where Francis first sang the Canticle of the Sun.

158 AN AVENUE OF OAKS NEAR LA FORESTA
This is the road to the present friary at La Foresta, where Francis stayed with the priest and worked the miracle of the vineyard.

159 THE CRYPT OF THE CATHEDRAL AT RIETI
The crypt is like a forest of pillars. The Cathedral was dedicated in 1157.

160 A FIREPLACE AT FONTE COLOMBO
It was here that the iron was heated when they cauterized the Saint's temples, and Francis of the courageous heart greeted "Brother Fire".

HIS LAST JOURNEY

Even when the spring came, Francis was no better. Cardinal Ugolino became very anxious and made arrangements for him to visit the most distinguished doctors at Siena. Francis therefore travelled through the hill-country of Tuscany and was received at Siena with great honour and reverence. A sudden hæmorrhage led everyone to think he was going to die, and the good priest Brother Benedict of Pirato was summoned. To him Francis dictated a message to the brethren: "Let this be my memorial, my blessing and my last testament: that they love one another as I have loved them and do love them now. Let them love and revere our dear Lady Poverty. Let them always be ready to serve faithfully and humbly all prelates and clergy of our holy mother the Church." Brother Elias was sent for, and he ordered that Francis should be brought to Assisi. The route was through Arezzo, Celle di Cortona, Gubbio, Nocera and Satriano to Assisi. The direct route by Perugia was deliberately avoided, for fear that if Francis was to die there, the people of Perugia would never let him be taken away. Assisi sent an armed escort to Satriano, to fetch him under their protection to Assisi, where the bishop took him into his house. The time for the general chapter at Pentecost arrived, but Francis was too weak to be able to take part. He dictated a letter, however, with his last recommendations to the brethren. During these last weeks very many of his sayings were recorded and treasured as precious relics. Meanwhile he was getting gradually weaker, and dropsy set in. One day Francis asked his good friend, the doctor, Buongiovanni: "Tell me, Bembegnate," he said affectionately, "what do you think about this dropsy?" The doctor answered evasively: "If it is God's will, you will recover." But Francis really wanted to know. "Well," said the doctor, "as far as medical science goes, there is no remedy, and I should think you will die at the end of September or early in October." Francis leaned back, raised his hands and said: "Welcome, Sister Death!" And his face lit up with joy. The gravity of the sickness increased, and soon Francis needed constant nursing. One of the brethren asked if he would rather have this death by illness, or the fierce death of martyrdom. Francis simply answered: "My son, I have always accepted as best and most pleasant whatever the Lord God arranges for me." When Brother Elias asked for his blessing, he laid his hand on him and said: "I bless you as much as I can, and more than I can; and what I cannot do, He who can do all things, will do for you." He then went on: "Farewell, all of you, my children; remain in the fear of God, and united to Him through His grace. Great trials will come upon you; serious troubles lie ahead. Blessed are those who will persevere in what they have begun. Terrible temptations will come and will lead many of you away. But I am now going to God, and before long I hope to be with my Lord, whom with all my heart I have served in my spirit."[58]

Notes on the four plates that follow

161 A PINNACLE OF THE CATHEDRAL OF SIENA

The cathedral was begun in 1284 and finished in 1382. Francis himself never saw this cathedral rising into the sky, but it was built during the springtime of Franciscan history.

162 THE HILL-COUNTRY BETWEEN SIENA AND AREZZO

This is the road of the dying Francis' journey home. There still lingers about this rolling countryside a breath of the sadness of that last journey.

163 AREZZO, THE CHURCH OF PIEVE DI SANTA MARIA

164 THE PORTA PERLICI AT ASSISI

Through this gateway Francis came home for the last time.

164

HIS DEATH

Francis wanted to die at his beloved Porziuncola, and the city, albeit unwillingly, consented to have the dying man transported there. He was carried out through the Portaccia Gate. Half-way down, near the hospice of the Crucigeri, he told the bearers to halt. They obeyed, and he turned his eyes, now so dim, towards the city of his youth, the city also of his many heavenly favours. And he blessed the city. "Lord," he said, "this was once a godless city. But You have favoured it and been merciful indeed. God bless you, sweet city: many souls have found salvation through you, many servants of the Most High will dwell in you, many will be chosen from you to enter the Kingdom of Heaven. Peace be with you." Then they went on towards the Porziuncola. During the last days he dictated to the brethren his will and testament, in which he once more gathered up the notions he had taught them by word and example, and the ideals which he always defended. When the feast of St Michael drew near, he asked for "Brother Jacoba" to be fetched to Assisi, bringing everything necessary for the burial: a grey cloth to go over the bier, a piece of linen for the face, a small cushion to go under the head, wax-candles, and finally a *mostacciuolo* (a kind of cake) "so that the body might share the present joy of the soul". Before, however, the messenger had set out for Rome to fetch "Brother Jacoba", she arrived at Assisi, bringing all the things he was asking for, and she was allowed to nurse him in his last hours. He also dictated a note of farewell to Sister Clare: "I, your little brother, Francis, declare my desire to follow the life in poverty of our most high Lord Jesus Christ and his most holy Mother, and to persevere in this desire to the end. I am asking you, my ladies, and I am recommending you, to remain true to this holy life of poverty and never to abandon it." When death was near, he bade them lay him on the bare earth, and then, with his left hand upon the wound in his side, he said: "I have done what I have had to do; may Christ teach you what you have to do." Then they borrowed fresh clothes for him and put them on him, and, praying, he waited for Sister Death to come. After sunset on October 3rd

[83]

1226 he died. In front of the door of the little cell a flight of larks appeared and rose into the sky, filling the evening air with song. The brethren stood round the lifeless body, and it appeared to them bathed in light; the face which had borne the marks of so much suffering now seemed clothed with angelic peace, while the limbs, long racked with pain, had become soft and supple; and the wounds shone like dark jewels on a white ground.[59]

At daybreak all the clergy of Assisi and crowds of people came to the Porziuncola. In solemn procession, singing songs of praise and waving palms, the people carried the Saint's body to the city. At San Damiano the choir-grille was opened, and Clare and the other nuns came weeping to the bier and venerated the stigmata. The funeral procession then went on again and the grille was closed once more. Never again could it open for so sorrowful an occasion.

The body was deposited for a time at San Giorgio, until the devotion of the Christian world had raised for the Saint a worthy monument.

Notes on the four plates that follow

165 SANTO STEFANO AT ASSISI
A pious tradition relates that the bells of this church rang of their own accord at the instant of the Saint's death.

166 TWO FINE CLOTHS
With these "Brother Jacoba" of Settesoli wiped the sweat from the brow of the dying Saint. They are now preserved at San Francesco at Assisi.

167 A CUSHION OF RED SILK, EMBROIDERED WITH GOLD
Upon this cushion the head of the Saint rested after his death.

168 A ROMANESQUE PROCESSIONAL CROSS OF SAN GIORGIO AT ASSISI
It was probably this cross that was carried at the head of St Francis' funeral procession. Behind the cross is an elaborate oriental cloth, which belonged to the treasury of San Giorgio, and may have been the one used to cover the bier during the procession. Both the cross and the cloth are now in the museum of the Sacro Convento at Assisi.

165 ▷

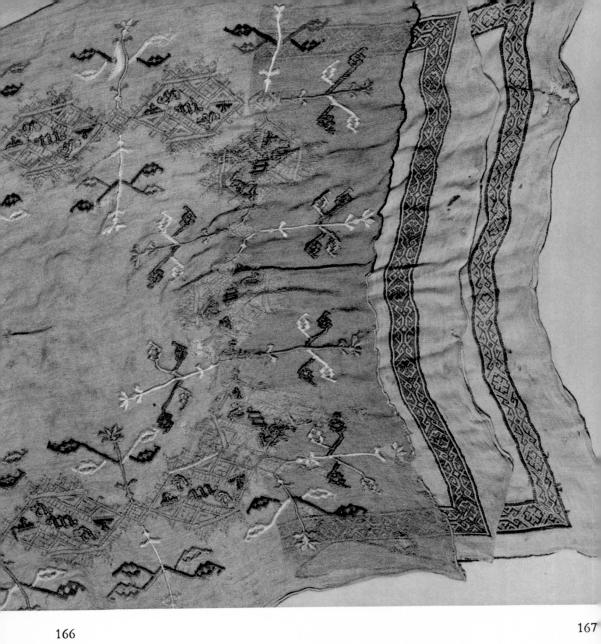

HIS TOMB

Soon the tomb of Francis became a centre of devotion and the scene of many miracles, so that Pope Gregory IX decided to extend the cult of the Saint to the whole world. On July 16th 1228, the Pope, whose court at the time was at Perugia, came to Assisi, accompanied by many dignitaries of the Church and an enormous crowd of the faithful. With great solemnity he declared Francis to be numbered among the saints.[60]

In the same year the foundation-stone of the great church was laid, which was to stand as a memorial above his tomb. Citizens of Assisi had given the land. Already in 1230 it was possible to bring the Saint's remains to rest in the new church. The procession was one of great splendour, and when they reached the church, so great were the crowds who wanted to see the body, and so anxious were the brethren that the precious relic should not be stolen, that Brother Elias, with armed assistance, removed the body from amid the tumult in the church. He then ordered the church to be cleared and the doors shut, and the body of the Saint was buried in secret. This secret burial gave rise to the rumour that it was not buried there at all, but in some inaccessible vault, with the hands raised to heaven.

But the matter was investigated in 1818, and the bones were found, simply laid within the bare rock. After this, the space round the tomb was opened out and turned into a chapel.

Today the tomb is the centre of unbroken veneration, and countless people go away richer in grace for having visited the tomb of the apostle of poverty.

Notes on the four plates that follow

The whole tomb has been protected by iron grilles.

Thomas of Celano was born about 1200, and at the age of fifteen had already joined Francis. One year after the Saint's death Thomas was commissioned by Pope Gregory IX to write the life of the Saint. He presented his completed work to the Pope on February 25th 1229. It is from this biography that the following description of the appearance of Francis is drawn.

"Francis was a man of ready speech and gay countenance, with good features. He was an unassuming man who did not know what cowardice was. He was of medium height, small rather than tall. He had a medium-sized and somewhat round-shaped head, and a rather long face. His forehead was flat and low. His eyes, of medium size, were black and clear-sighted. His hair was dark and his eyebrows level. His nose was regular, delicate and straight. His ears stood out somewhat, but were small, and his temples were flat. He had a sharp and fiery, but most winning way of speaking; and his voice was strong, clear and musical, and pleasant to hear. His teeth were white, regular and unspoiled; and his lips were narrow but very gentle. He had a black and not very abundant beard. His neck was slim, his shoulders level; and he had short arms, delicate hands with long fingers and somewhat pointed nails. His legs were slender and his feet notably small. He had a delicate skin and was very thin. He wore a rough habit, allowed himself very little sleep, and above all his hand was ever generous."[61]

The first proper portraits of the New Painting occupied themselves with Francis. The people wanted to have the likeness of their beloved Saint. The oldest of these pictures is, according to present opinion, the fresco at the Sacro Speco at Subiaco (Plate 173). It was apparently painted, by an unknown hand, two years after the death of St Francis, and it corresponds in almost everything, except for the fair hair, to the description given by Thomas of Celano. It seems as if the painter actually knew St Francis.

A painting on wood of the 13th century in the Franciscan museum at Santa Maria degli Angeli, was, according to ancient tradition, painted by Cimabue on the wooden cover of the sarcophagus. Here for the first time the wound in the side is shown. The face is depicted extremely long, the hair is brown, and the capuce is thrown back round the neck (Plate 174).

Berlinghieri, in the picture painted about 1260 and often copied, shows a very ascetic and emaciated man with the stigmata (Plate 175). This painting is now in the museum of the Conventuals at San Francesco at Assisi.

The famous portrait of the Saint with the Madonna and angels, by Cimabue, in the lower church of San Francesco was overpainted in the Baroque period. But, nevertheless, the small features generally correspond with the statement of Celano (Plate 176).

The most convincing and outstanding portrait is the one we have selected for the jacket of this book, and it opened the way to that lyrical sweetness that became characteristic of subsequent Franciscan art. The painting was at one time attributed to Simone Martini of Siena, but is now believed to be the work of Donato of Siena.

Notes on the four plates that follow, and on the picture on the jacket

173 THE MOST ANCIENT PORTRAIT OF THE SAINT
Painted in 1228, two years after his death, on the wall of a side-chapel at the Sacro Speco at Subiaco.

174 13TH-CENTURY PORTRAIT
Alleged to have been painted by Cimabue on the wooden cover of the Saint's sarcophagus. (Museum of the friary at Santa Maria degli Angeli.)

175 PORTRAIT OF ST FRANCIS BY BERLINGHIERI
Painted in 1260, 34 years after the Saint's death. (Museum at San Francesco, Assisi.)

176 PORTRAIT OF THE SAINT BY CIMABUE
About 1280, but heavily overpainted. (Lower church at San Francesco, Assisi.)

PICTURE ON THE JACKET
A portrait of Francis, previously attributed to Simone Martini, but now with more probability to Donato of Siena. (Fresco in the lower church at San Francesco, Assisi.)

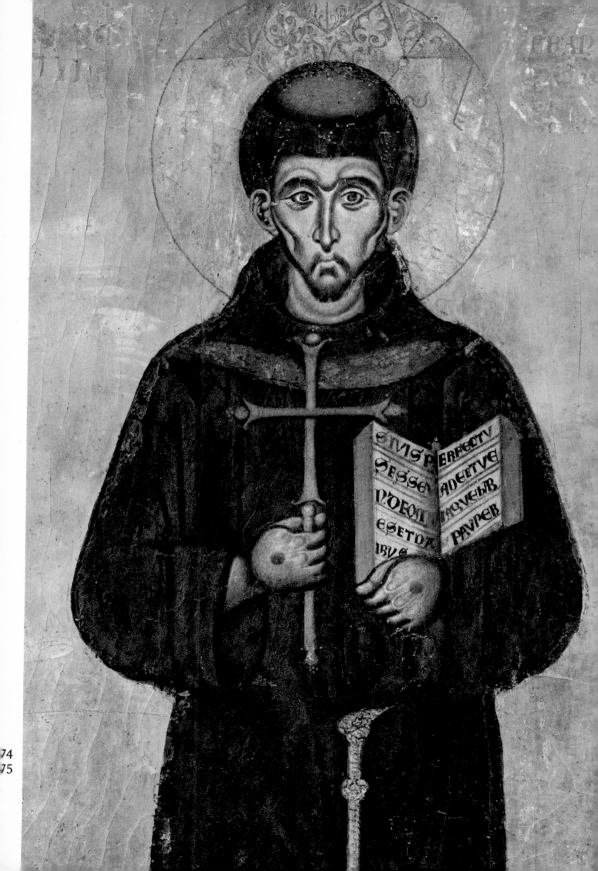

THE CHURCH OF SAN FRANCESCO

The mighty basilica that enshrines the tomb of St Francis at Assisi has in every age aroused both disapproval and admiration: disapproval, because the massive and magnificent work of Brother Elias seems in no way to accord with the Saint's ideal of poverty; and admiration, because its architectural and artistic conception has become the most perfect and powerful expression of the whole Franciscan spirit.

When seen, not so much as a place of prayer but as a mighty fortress of God, the basilica rises at the western end of the town, and seems, especially when viewed from the plain, to be trailing the little town clinging to the slopes of Monte Subasio, and bringing all its little sanctuaries with it. It is the focal point of the town now.

Elias of Assisi, later known as Elias of Cortona after his burial there, was as much as Francis a child of his time. It was an age of magnificence, and it was natural, perhaps, that Elias should desire to build a shrine as magnificent as the Father's sanctity was magnificent. Thus there arose not one church, but two; a huge friary with cloistered walks, and towers to the number of the apostles, surmounted by a lordly campanile, with a play of stairways of the most graceful design; a mass of frescoes on wall and ceiling that utterly overwhelm the beholder. In the crypt beneath he finds the tomb of the Saint protected by the unadorned bulk of the rock-like walls; he mounts to the lower church to find the dark rhythm of the low romanesque vault; and he then emerges into the clear daylight of the upper church with its high gothic arches enclosing the sunlit space. Nothing certain is known of the architect, though a certain James of Germany is sometimes named. Three schools of painters contributed to the immortal decoration of this place: there is Cimabue and his School, then Giotto and his School, and finally the School of Siena. It was here in the vaulting of this church that a movement was born that is known as the New Painting. Thus Francis in his own life began a new kind of piety and Christian living, through his "Canticle of the Sun" he opened a new era in the poetry of Italy, and through his basilica arose a new period in the history of art.

In general, it may be said that Cimabue's frescoes are characterized by a certain seriousness: there is nothing trivial, every detail is important, and here for the first time in Christian art something of the emotions of the heart is portrayed. The name of Giotto is perhaps even greater. He was a tertiary. And here we find seriousness portrayed with an easy grace: the stylized becomes personal: painting becomes Franciscan! We find here a true dramatic gift, the perfect presentation of a story, and a feeling that every detail has its essential part in the drama. Giotto could somehow paint the very feelings of his subjects, and paint them true to life in the real essentials.

With the School of Siena a new lyrical feeling is born. Here the poetry of Jacopone da Todi, a Franciscan contemporary, finds its expression in paint. San Francesco at Assisi is in some sort a summary of all the beauty of the Franciscan spirit.

Notes on the eight plates that follow

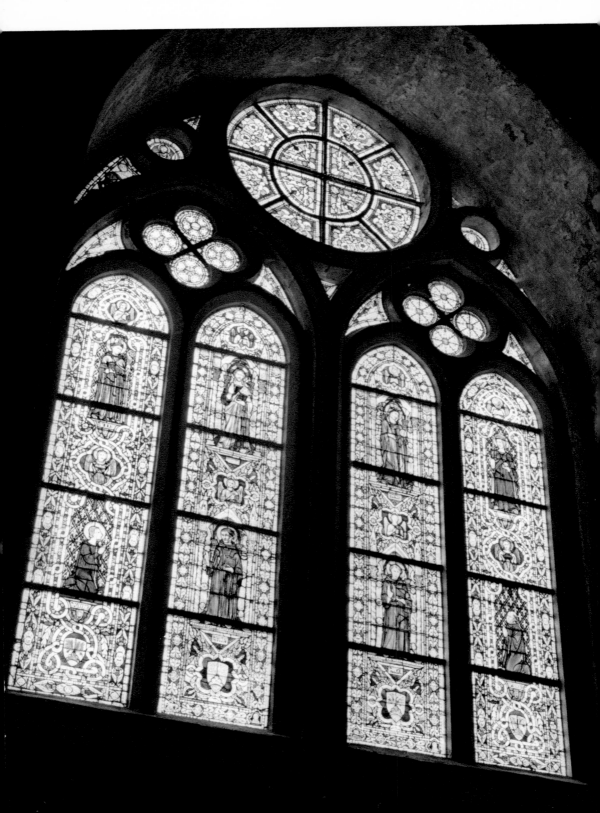

180

181

182 >
183 >

184

THE SACRO CONVENTO

The Sacro Convento looks like a mighty ship sailing westwards upon the heaving waves of the Umbrian landscape. And those astonishing arches in regular series, supporting the Order's greatest treasure, seem to grow out of the hillside and, like a cliff, form a spur of the hill itself.

The basilica was begun almost at once after the death of St Francis; adjoining it is the huge friary, the Sacro Convento, that during the centuries has been many times rebuilt and extended. It was the Franciscan Pope Sixtus IV who contributed more than any other to the building, and his statue stands at the south-west corner imparting his blessing to the whole countryside.

Within the rows of arches, facing the plain, are long gothic-vaulted galleries, which give wonderful views over the surrounding country. A two-storied gallery also surrounds the small cloister-garth inside, the Chiostro dei Morti, where are buried the Order's superiors and special friends from earliest times. There is a huge refectory, whose dimensions are almost those of the campanile: across the end-wall is a Last Supper by Solimene, and along the side-walls are paintings of those Popes who had specially close ties with the Order. The cloister of Sixtus IV, built in the Lombard style of the 15th century, is decorated with a Life of the Saint by Dono Donis.

In 1866 the friary was seized by the state and turned into a school. But in 1929 the Lateran Treaty between Pope Pius XI and Mussolini restored the building to the Conventual Franciscans, who now with loving care look after the Sacro Convento, "the mother and head of all Franciscan houses".

Notes on the four plates that follow

185

186 >
187 >

188

THE FRANCISCAN ORDER

The immediate concern of those who came just after Francis was to set before the world in visible form the ideals bequeathed to them by the founder. It was first of all Assisi that was seized with the enthusiasm born of St Francis. Franciscan voices were soon heard in all Assisi and in all the land of Umbria, and the Sacro Convento, the great work of Brother Elias, stood there as a fortress to guard the ideal. In the plain below, a great basilica rose above the little chapel of the Porziuncola, protecting the hallowed spot and sheltering the crowds of pilgrims who came to visit it. Next to the basilica is the large friary of the Friars Minor, who preserve the memory of the Saint in the place made holy by his death.

In the middle of the town is the convent of the Poor Clares, where is preserved the body of St Clare, the great lady who struggled so hard to keep the legacy of poverty left to her by St Francis. Scattered in the neighbourhood of the town are those hidden holy places which Francis loved so much, just because they are hidden and because their only adornment is their evangelical simplicity: San Damiano, the Carceri and Rivotorto. In these places the spirit of Francis is strongly alive.

Gradually the whole of Italy was captured by the power of the Franciscan movement, and people were saying: "All Italy is putting on the habit!" But it was not only Italy. The brethren with their message of poverty were crossing the Alps and voyaging across the seas. The Franciscan ideal was being preached to new people, in new places and in other times. And every ideal is always in danger of being betrayed. Here and there in these new circumstances the ideal became obscured; but there were always men who arose and sought their inspiration from the rock-tomb of the founder on the "hill of paradise", or from the Porziuncola, or Rivotorto, or the Carceri; and thus the Franciscan movement, at first like a grain of mustard seed, grew into a mighty tree with many branches.

And these are the names of the branches:

Of the First Order	Friars Minor or Franciscans (O.F.M.)	24 993 friars
	Conventuals (O.F.M. Conv.)	3 650 friars
	Capuchins (O.F.M. Cap.)	14 179 friars
Of the Second Order	Poor Clares	about 13 000 nuns
Of the Third Order	Living in community:	men about 1 000 religious
		women about 100 000 sisters
		(in over 160 Congregations)

Living in the world: about $3\frac{1}{2}$ million tertiaries, men and women.[62]

And "the birds of the air come and dwell in the branches thereof". The saints who have dwelt in the branches of the tree of Francis include martyrs and doctors of the Church, kings and beggars—all of whom, for the love of God, made themselves poor. Learned men and artists, Popes and bold seafaring men, all kinds of people have taken the Cord of the Poverello: and still today there are thousands mature in the spirit of Francis, and thousands again still growing to maturity, whose only ideal is to live in the manner of the Gospel of Jesus Christ, in the poverty and love of Francis of Assisi.

The words of the young prisoner at Perugia, still bent on acquiring worldly fame, have come true: "I know for certain that one day all the world will do me homage."

Notes on the four plates that follow

189 THE CONVENT OF SANTA CHIARA AT ASSISI

190 A SON OF ST FRANCIS

191 THE CHAPEL OF THE PORZIUNCOLA IN THE BASILICA OF SANTA MARIA DEGLI ANGELI

192 THE APOTHEOSIS OF THE FRANCISCAN ORDER
A gobelin of Flemish workmanship, now in the museum of San Francesco at Assisi. It was given to the friary by Pope Sixtus IV in 1479 and it represents the most glorious flowers that sprang from the root of Francis.

190 >
191 >

192

ASSISI, HOLY CITY

The course of Italian poetry, after St Francis' "Canticle of the Sun", rose suddenly to the supreme height of the Divina Commedia of the Tertiary, Dante Alighieri. The poet greets Assisi:

> Di quella costa, là dov' ella frange
> Più sua rattezza, nacque al mondo un Sole,
> Come fa questo talvolta di Gange.
> Però chi d'esso loco fa parole,
> Non dica Ascesi, chè direbbe corto,
> Ma Oriente, se proprio dir vuole.   (Par. XI. 49–54)

> From this same slope, just where it breaks away
> Most gently, to the world was born a sun,
> As this from Ganges on a summer's day.
> Therefore, whene'er the place is named, let none
> Call it "Ascesi"—word of meagre sense;
> But "Orient" should its title rightly run.   (Tr. Bickersteth)

The whole of Assisi is the shrine of Francis, who though dead more than 700 years, still lives in the hearts of thousands.

Before his time, Assisi was one of those many small towns of Italy, alternately elated and consumed by petty strife and jealousy, with a brief heroic period in the age of chivalry and a chequered history in local war. The citizens' only ideals were to outrival their neighbours either in military strength or in mercantile success.

Then came Francis, son of the merchant Pietro Bernardone, at first one like the rest, but then gradually by God's grace acquiring an insight into the true values of these things. Gradually the people of Assisi began to absorb his spirit, and before long Lady Poverty was dragging men and women out of their palaces or their shops, and inspiring boys and girls with new dreams of greatness. The names of Francis and of Clare were on everyone's lips, and gradually almost every street had its memory of their sacred folly: churches and houses, even stables and gardens bore the impress of his passage, and all Assisi became his memorial. Assisi has but a single song to sing, and that song is about Francis. The world cannot have enough of it, and the name of Francis is the only echo that the traveller brings away.

Since the dying Saint from the plain below turned his eyes, now so dim, towards the holy city and blessed it, Franciscan song has never ceased to raise its voice to bless that holy place.

194 >
195 >

200

MAPS

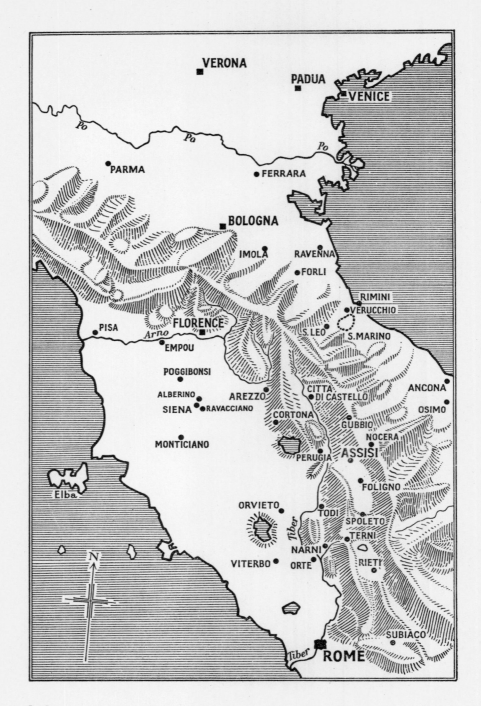

VERONA

PADUA

VENICE

Po

Po

Po

PARMA

FERRARA

BOLOGNA

IMOLA

RAVENNA

FORLI

RIMINI

VERUCCHIO

PISA

Arno

FLORENCE

S.LEO

S.MARINO

EMPOLI

POGGIBONSI

CITTA
DI CASTELLO

ANCONA

ALBERINO

AREZZO

SIENA

RAVACCIANO

CORTONA

OSIMO

GUBBIO

NOCERA

MONTICIANO

PERUGIA

ASSISI

FOLIGNO

Elba

ORVIETO

Tiber

TODI

SPOLETO

TERNI

N

NARNI

VITERBO

ORTE

RIETI

SUBIACO

Tiber

ROME

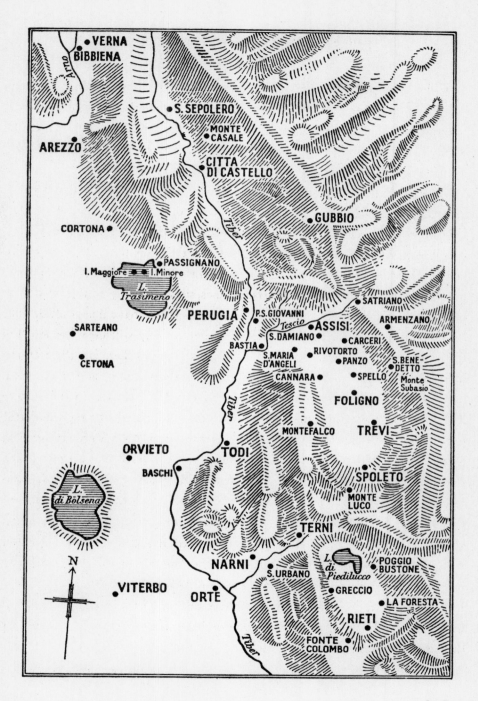

EPILOGUE BY THE PHOTOGRAPHER

The object of this book has been to provide authentic pictures to illustrate the life of St Francis of Assisi. I consider it particularly valuable that these photographs generally reflect as far as possible the actual world in which the Saint lived. Of course, this cannot be so quite literally, since things will have changed much during 700 years, but all the same, in spite of many difficulties, I have tried to allow modern equipment to take here and there a genuine glance back into medieval times.

I photographed places which the Saint visited, churches in which he prayed foundations which he made, houses in which he stayed, and things which were connected with him and which are now treasured as relics. Where these things were impossible, I have limited myself to landscapes, since, after all, the smooth hills of central Italy, and the green plains with their grey olives can have changed little since his time, and among men and animals there can have been still less alteration. To-day, white oxen still draw the simple plough as they did then, and the brethren of St Francis still ride the same good donkeys on their rounds, as they did then. On the way I had many joys of new discovery. For instance, in the remote little friary of the Capuchins at Monte Casale, I stumbled upon a wonderful romanesque Madonna (Plate 74), which was apparently a gift from a nobleman, to St Francis, and before which he would therefore have said a prayer. The statue has been decorated in the baroque period, so that its venerable age and priceless value might easily have gone undetected. I was the first person to photograph it. And then there is the majestic figure surrounded by sun, moon and stars, in the centre of the altar-piece at Città di Castello (Plate 153); is it not legitimate to suppose that it inspired the Canticle of the Sun, since just before its composition Francis was passing through the town?

I would like here to thank the many people who so kindly helped me while on my travels, and made it possible for me to make this collection of pictures for the Life of St Francis.

LEONARD VON MATT

EPILOGUE BY THE WRITER

This book is a picture book. After the many biographies of St Francis, from Thomas of Celano to Father Cuthbert, there was no need to write another. But the purpose of the text of this book is to tell the story that lies behind the photographs, and to place the pictures in their proper setting in the Saint's life.

The writer has not attempted to say anything new about St Francis, and still less to enter into any of the learned historical controversies: he would have felt like David in Saul's armour, quite unable to give battle.

For these reasons actual quotations from the sources have rarely been used, and an attempt has only been made to capture their sense and spirit. The writer will therefore be happy if by the simple words of this book the reader has learnt something more about Francis, and has been further inspired to walk in his footsteps, with something of that sweet gaiety of the Saint's song in his heart and on his lips.

WALTER HAUSER
Tertiary

INDEX OF THE PLATES
(Numbers refer to the plates)

FOOTNOTE REFERENCES
to printed biographies of St Francis

(Refs to Fr Cuthbert's *Life* are given according to the original English, ed. 1914, while the others refer to a German text)

1 Karrer, p. 33
2 Jörgensen, p. 138
3 Jörgensen, p. 141
4 Jörgensen, p. 148
5 Karrer, p. 135
6 Jörgensen, p. 150
7 Cuthbert, p. 18
8 Cuthbert, p. 21
9 Cuthbert, p. 22
10 Cuthbert, p. 24
11 Cuthbert, p. 28
12 Cuthbert, p. 29
13 Cuthbert, p. 33
14 Cuthbert, p. 34
15 Cuthbert, p. 40
16 Cuthbert, p. 44
17 Karrer, p. 451
18 Jörgensen, p. 206
19 Cuthbert, p. 49
20 Cuthbert, p. 52
21 Schnürer, p. 31
22 Schnürer, p. 33
23 Karrer, p. 61
24 Cuthbert, p. 98
25 Karrer, p. 74
26 Cuthbert, p. 125
27 Karrer, p. 161
28 Karrer, p. 163
29 Karrer, p. 397
30 Karrer, p. 431
31 Karrer, p. 164
32 Cuthbert, p. 188

33 Karrer, p. 100
34 Celano, p. 268
35 Celano, p. 68
36 Celano, p. 175
37 Maritain, *Terres Franciscaines*
38 Felder, p. 144
39 Cuthbert, p. 269
40 Karrer, p. 441
41 Cuthbert, p. 269
42 Cuthbert, p. 337
43 Karrer, p. 181
44 Karrer, p. 199
45 Cuthbert, p. 303
46 Cuthbert, p. 380–383
47 Cuthbert, p. 385
48 Cuthbert, p. 392
49 Cuthbert, 396
50 Karrer, p. 125
51 Jörgensen, *Pilgerbuch*, p. 19
52 Karrer, p. 269
53 Life of Brother Leo (in *Analecta Franciscana*, Quaracchi, 1897/67)
54 Jörgensen, *Pilgerbuch*, p. 329
55 Karrer, p. 705
56 Jörgensen, p. 508
57 Karrer, p. 674
58 Cuthbert, p. 446
59 Celano, p. 110
60 Celano, p. 311
61 Celano, p. 87
62 *Annuario Pontificio*, 1951.

A SHORT BIBLIOGRAPHY

Abate, P. G., *La casa dove nacque San Francesco.* 1941.

Abate, P. G., *Storia e Leggenda intorno alla nascita di San Francesco.* 1949.

Bastianini-Frei, *Das Lied der Armut.* 1947.

Casutt, L., *Das Erbe eines grossen Herzens.* 1949.

Christen-Felder, *Leben des hl. Franz von Assisi.* 1944.

Cuthbert-Widlöcher, *Der hl. Franz von Assisi.* 1944.

 (German translation of Fr Cuthbert, *Life of St Francis of Assisi,* first published 1912).

Errani, G., *Assisi.* 1951.

Grillantini, C., *Osimo sacra*

Guby, R., *Assisi.* 1925.

Jacobelli, P. G., *Patriae Lux. San Francisco di Assisi.* 1940.

Jörgensen, J., *Der hl. Franziskus von Assisi,* 1944.

Jörgensen, J., *Das Pilgerbuch.* 1908.

Karrer, Otto, *Franz von Assisi.* 1945.

Leopoldo da Cortona, *Il primo Convento Francescano.* 1914.

Nediani, T., *Montecasale.* 1915.

Schnürer, Gustav, *Franz von Assisi.* 1905.

Thode, Henry, *Franz von Assisi.* 1934.

Thomas of Celano, *Leben und Wundertaten des hl. Franziskus von Assisi.* 1925.

 (German translation of the first biography)

Venuti de Dominicis, *La "Croce Santa" di Cortona.*

Zocca, Emma, *Assisi.* 1949.

PREVIOUS WORKS BY THE SAME AUTHORS

LEONARD VON MATT

Rom. A Standard work in two volumes with a total of 600 pages of pictures
Vol. I "Die Kunst in Rom" Vol. II "Papsttum und Vatikan" (Art in Rome;
Papacy and Vatican)
Collaborators on the text: Dr Dieter von Balthasar, Mgr Paul Krieg, Fr Beatus Ambord. 1950

Die Päpstliche Schweizergarde (The Papal Swiss Guards). 56 pages of pictures,
with text by the Chaplain of the Guards, Mgr Paul Krieg. 1948

Der Heilige Bruder Klaus. The official handbook for the canonization of St Nicholas von Flüe.
56 pages of photographs by Leonard von Matt.
Text by the Bruderklausen-Kaplan Werner Durrer, and J. K. Scheuber. 1947

Uri. A book of photographs of the land of Uri. With text by various hands. 1946

WALTER HAUSER

Via Crucis. A little book of Stations of the Cross, with illustrations by Willy Helbing. 1947
Singendes Gleichnis (A parable of song). Poems. 2nd ed., 1947
Stufen zum Licht (The stairway of light). Poems. 4th ed., 1948
Das ewige Siegel (The eternal seal). Poems. 1950

Here is a life story shown through unusually vivid and outstanding photographs. Leonard von Matt, the noted Swiss photographer, has fashioned a living biography of a man who died more than 700 years ago, reconstructing his life from the landscape in which the Saint lived and various places and things connected with him. A sound historical sense together with an artist's intuition produced this collection of studies. Churches in which Saint Francis prayed, Friaries which he founded, houses where he stayed and objects which he used were photographed. Sometimes there were no direct memories of him—but the landscape is always there : the smooth hills of Central Italy and the green plains with their grey olives and, still more, men and animals, have changed little since his time. In a way this book is at the same time a song of praise of that Italian earth which has produced such great saints and such supreme works of art.

Yet this is also a book to be read. The text tells the story along with the photographs, and places them in their proper historical setting. Father Hauser writes with a beautiful simplicity almost biblical in its measured pace and directness—a style singularly appropriate for a study of St. Francis, which is most successfully preserved in Father Bullough's English version and happily matched with the spirit of the Franciscan springtime caught in the almost miraculous beauty of 200 superb pictures.